FIGHTING DIVISIONS

FIGHTING DIVISIONS

HISTORIES OF EACH U.S. ARMY COMBAT DIVISION
IN WORLD WAR II

By

Chief Warrant Officer E. J. Kahn, Jr.

and

Technical Sergeant Henry McLemore

From materials provided by the Office of Technical Information, Special Information Section, Headquarters Army Ground Forces.

ZENGER PUBLISHING CO., INC.
P.O. BOX 9883 • WASHINGTON, D.C. 20015

Library of Congress Cataloging in Publication Data:

Kahn, Ely Jacques, 1916-
    Fighting divisions.

    "From materials provided by the Office of
Technical Information, Special Information Section,
Headquarters Army Ground Forces."
    Reprint of the 1946 ed. published by Infantry
Journal Press, Washington.
    1. United States. Army--History--World War,
1939-1945. 2. World War, 1939-1945--United States.
I. McLemore, Henry, joint author. II. Title.
D769.1.K3 1979   940.54'12'73   79-18378
ISBN 0-89201-058-4

Printed in the United States of America

CONTENTS

1st Division

2nd Division

3rd Division

4th Division

5th Division

6th Division

7th Division

8th Division

9th Division

10th Division

11th Airborne Division

13th Airborne Division

17th Airborne Division

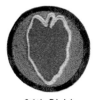

24th Division

25th Division

26th Division

27th Division

28th Division

29th Division

30th Division

31st Division

32nd Division

33rd Division

34th Division

35th Division

36th Division

37th Division

38th Division

40th Division

41st Division

42nd Division

43rd Division

44th Division

45th Division

63rd Division

65th Division

66th Division

69th Division

70th Division

71st Division

75th Division

76th Division

77th Division

78th Division

79th Division

80th Division

81st Division

82nd Airborne Division

83rd Division

84th Division

85th Division

86th Division

87th Division

88th Division

89th Division

90th Division

91st Division

92nd Division

93rd Division

94th Division

95th Division

96th Division

97th Division

98th Division

99th Division

100th Division

101st Airborne Division

102nd Division

103rd Division

104th Division

106th Division

Americal Division

Philippine Division

1st Cavalry Division

1st Armored Division

2nd Armored Division

3rd Armored Division

4th Armored Division

5th Armored Division

6th Armored Division

7th Armored Division

8th Armored Division

9th Armored Division

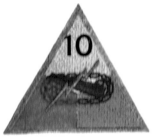

10th Armored Division

11th Armored Division

12th Armored Division

13th Armored Division

14th Armored Division

16th Armored Division

20th Armored Division

PREFACE

As COMMANDING GENERAL of the 6th Army Group in Europe, I considered it my responsibility to be constantly informed of the activities of each fighting division assigned to my command. As informative battle reports arrived in my headquarters, I often considered both the advisability and desirability of immediately releasing accounts of impressive battle achievements to American citizens at home so that they, too, might be cognizant of the ever-growing record of success of these basic Army Ground Forces fighting units.

Unfortunately, however, public release of such accomplishments at that time would have furnished the enemy with information which would have been of invaluable assistance to him, and we were required, therefore, to observe caution in our published tributes. Now that the war has been concluded successfully and restrictions on the battle participation of our troops have been lifted, the daring exploits of our divisions can be published.

To my knowledge, this book is the first attempt to cover the history of every division that comprised our ground combat forces. The battleground of these divisions encompassed the entire world and the battles they fought were won the hard way, step by step, and yard by yard. Every step over every yard meant a risk for some unheralded foot-soldier; and for every mile gained a heavy price was paid, not only in money and material, but in pain, and fear, and flowing blood.

The men of the divisions and attached units that contributed so much to our victories should never have cause to doubt that the debt we owe them is a large one, or that we can ever pay it in full.

JACOB L. DEVERS
General
Commanding General
Army Ground Forces

INTRODUCTION

No SOLDIER'S PATCH is worn with greater pride than that displayed on the shoulder of a man who has belonged to a combat division. In World War II, as in every past war, the major share of our fighting has been borne by our ground troops, particularly those of the Infantry. Most of our Infantrymen belong to divisions, which are our Army's principal combat teams, composed of soldiers who are trained and expected to do one primary job—fight. In a huge army made up of seemingly bewildering groups of specialists—an army in which the soldiers who actually come to grips with the enemy must of necessity be a distinct minority—our divisions hold a unique position. They are the Army's fighting core, and whatever any other forces do is largely preliminary or supporting to their actions.

Most of the combat ground soldiers who have already returned from theaters of operations, and most of those not yet home, wear a divisional shoulder patch. They will rightly expect the citizens for whom they have sacrificed so much to know something about what they have done and what the organizations in which they have served have done. It is manifestly impossible for any person to hope to become familiar in detail with the accomplishments of all our Army divisions, or to be able instantly to recognize every one of their elaborately varied shoulder insignia.

But a little learning is no longer a dangerous thing. Earlier in the war, largely for security reasons, much information about divisional achievements could not be released until it was old and apt to be buried under the steady flow of livelier news. For those members of the public who have tried diligently to keep abreast of the progress of our fighting units, the task has usually been difficult and often impossible. American citizens at home can thus readily absolve themselves of any charge that they have been inexcusably indifferent toward the battle accomplishments of any particular group of soldiers. Such a defense, however, may carry little weight with a returning combat veteran, who has spent one, two, or three years abroad as a fighting member of a division, thinks it is the best damn division in the world, and may want to make something of it if you don't agree.

You had better agree.

Today, pride in divisional achievements, and knowledge of them, need no longer be limited to the select fraternity of the division itself. Secrecy is not a governing factor, any more, in any recitation of the deeds of divisions that fought in any theater of the war. For those who want to know them the facts are available.

This book is not a complete history of our combat divisions. It is, rather, an attempt to assemble for the first time enough material on every one of our divisions to give the average citizen a brief idea of where each has been and what each has done. Some of our divisions have had many months' more battle experience than others, and space has made it necessary to restrict the account of their accomplishments to the bare minimum. Wherever possible, this material has been based on historical reports prepared by the divisions themselves. In some cases, the available source material has been regrettably skimpy. In several cases, it has been noted that two or more divisions have set forth virtually identical claims for a single objective. The explanation, of course, is that frequently more than one division has attacked more than one city or defense line, and that divisional historians have shown understandable partisanship toward their own outfits. This book tries to be fair to all divisions, but it may inadvertently have hurt the feelings of a particular unit by neglecting to mention some achievement of which the division itself is especially proud. It would have taken an inordinate amount of time to check each division's story with the division concerned, and the editors have therefore been obliged to fall back on official records and on the testimony of officers and men familiar through personal experience with the divisions' histories.

Divisions fight on the ground, and it is there that our lasting gains in this war have been scored, our major victories won, most of our heroes spawned, and most of our casualties suffered. Sixty-four per cent of the Army's Medals of Honor and seventy-five per cent of its casualties have been earned by Infantrymen—and yet only one out of every five soldiers is an Infantryman. These statistics are the measure of the foot soldier's unparalleled risks and unparalleled deeds, and nearly all our foot soldiers have fought as members of combat divisions.

It would be unjust, however, not to mention here those thousands of ground soldiers who have performed notably in combat as members of separate task forces, regiments, battalions, and other non-divisional units. Most of these have been artillery, tank, cavalry, antiaircraft, or combat engineer men, serving under direct control of corps or armies, or sometimes attached to, though not actually assigned to, divisions. Others of these soldiers have been Infantrymen—some of the best the Army has. The 100th Infantry Battalion, for instance, later a part of the 442nd Regimental Combat Team, contained the famous Japanese-American fighters whose record in action in Italy and France should be known to all other Americans. There have been the six Ranger battalions, spearheads of attacks in Europe and the Philippines. The long list includes the 1st Special Service Force, a picked group of Canadians and Americans who operated in Italy; Merrill's Marauders and the Mars Task Force, of Burma fame; and dozens of other small units.

By far the greater part of our combat ground forces, however, have been assigned to divisions. After the fall of Bataan, our combat Army consisted of 89 of them—one cavalry, one mountain, five airborne, 16 armored, and 66 infantry. Most of them are relatively new. On August 3, 1940, when the Army began to expand with the establishment of a General Headquarters under the War Department, our ground forces were pitifully small. As a fighting nucleus, the United States had eight Regular Army infantry divisions, all considerably under strength; one armored division, barely out of the experimental stage; and a little more than one cavalry division. There were no airborne divisions at all, and, even by the summer of 1941, our total complement of paratroopers consisted of exactly one battalion. Many divisions which are by now veterans of extremely arduous combat existed only on paper when the Japs struck at Pearl Harbor on December 7, 1941. All our divisions are numbered, with two exceptions—the Philippine and the Americal. Armored divisions have their own numerical sequence. Infantry, airborne, and mountain divisions are in another sequence, divided into three parts. The lowest numbers are those of the so-called Regular divisions—usually composed chiefly of selectees but built on a framework of experienced prewar personnel. The middle group of numbers—from 26 through 45—are those of the National Guard divisions. The rest are those of divisions activated during the national emergency for war service only, a number of which, however, fought in World War I, then became inactive, and were built up again for the Army of World War II.

At the start of this war the only divisions upon which the War Department could depend for reasonably immediate battle service were the Regular and Guard outfits. The latter had begun to go on active duty in September 1940. Though the National Guard has been the subject of much controversial talk, in and out of the Army, the fact remains that without our Guard divisions we simply would not have been able to conduct our early operations in the Pacific and Mediterranean Theaters. The first all-Selective-Service divisions to see action, the 85th and 88th, did not start fighting until the spring of 1944—more than a year and a half after our older divisions had gone into action. It was the Guard divisions—the 27th, 32nd, 34th, 36th, 37th, 41st, and 45th, to name a few—which, along with such Regular outfits as the 1st, 3d, 7th and 9th Infantry and the 1st and 2nd Armored Divisions, did the bulk of our Army's fighting early in the war.

These veteran outfits have, accordingly, suffered most heavily. It is commonly thought, for instance, that an infantry division has about 15,000 people in it. That is more or less so *at any one time*. But through transfers and, principally, battle casualties, some of our old divisions have had many times that number of men pass through their ranks and thus become eligible to wear the division insignia on one shoulder or the other—left shoulder for those presently assigned, and right for alumni. One single regiment of the 45th Division (the normal strength of a regiment is roughly 3,000 men) has had some 25,000 men assigned to it alone since its activation five years ago. As of April 30, 1945, the three divisions with the highest number of casualties of any in the Army were, understandably, among the group of outfits longest tested in battle—the 3d, 45th and 36th Infantry Divisions, with respective casualty totals of 34,224, 27,554 and 27,344. Remember—the strength of a division is only some 15,000 men. It is interesting to note that these three divisions were the ones that spearheaded the Seventh Army's invasion of Southern France on August 15, 1944.

Our modern infantry divisions are considerably streamlined versions of their World War I forerunners. In the earlier war, when mobility was a less desirable asset than mass, divisions were "square" (being built around two infantry brigades of two regiments each) and relatively cumbersome. In the peacetime years, the War Department began to experiment with a radically different division—a triangular one fashioned around three infantry regiments. For a while, the 2nd Infantry Division was assigned the role of military guinea pig, and in 1937, while temporily triangularized, it made a move by motor so unprecedentedly swift that observers were amazed. (This was back in the pre-atomic days when observers were more easily amazed.) Regular Army divisions were subsequently triangularized, and a few months after the National Guard divisions, originally square, were federalized, each lost one of its four infantry regiments and went through other changes, such as shifting from a brigade of field artillery to four battalions. Some of the infantry regiments so detached went on to establish distinguished combat records on their own. The 158th Infantry, for example, initially part of the 45th Division, was shipped to Panama for training, there adopted the nickname of the "Bushmasters," and eventually saw combat in New Britain, New Guinea, and the Philippines.

The infantry division, first formed in 1917, is the oldest and most prominent divisional organization. Its present make-up is triangular down to and including its tiniest unit—the rifle squad. The division's principal striking power (see next two pages) consists of three regiments, each one of three battalions and supporting troops, each battalion in turn of three rifle companies and support, each company of three rifle platoons and support, and each platoon, finally, of three squads. Every group of foot soldiers has its own supporting fire. A regiment fights as part of a combat team, assisted by a battalion of light field artillery in addition to its own cannon and antitank units. A battalion has its own heavy-weapons company, and a company its own weapons platoon. Even the rifle squad has its own

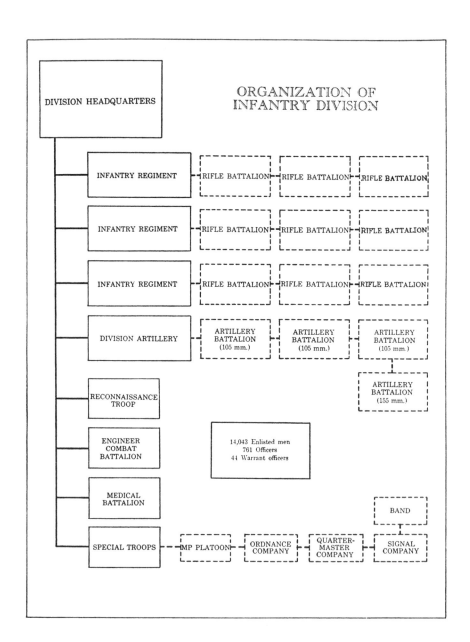

ORGANIZATION OF
INFANTRY DIVISION

DIVISION HEADQUARTERS

INFANTRY REGIMENT — RIFLE BATTALION — RIFLE BATTALION — RIFLE BATTALION

INFANTRY REGIMENT — RIFLE BATTALION — RIFLE BATTALION — RIFLE BATTALION

INFANTRY REGIMENT — RIFLE BATTALION — RIFLE BATTALION — RIFLE BATTALION

DIVISION ARTILLERY — ARTILLERY BATTALION (105 mm.) — ARTILLERY BATTALION (105 mm.) — ARTILLERY BATTALION (105 mm.)

ARTILLERY BATTALION (155 mm.)

RECONNAISSANCE TROOP

ENGINEER COMBAT BATTALION

14,043 Enlisted men
761 Officers
44 Warrant officers

MEDICAL BATTALION

BAND

SPECIAL TROOPS — MP PLATOON — ORDNANCE COMPANY — QUARTER-MASTER COMPANY — SIGNAL COMPANY

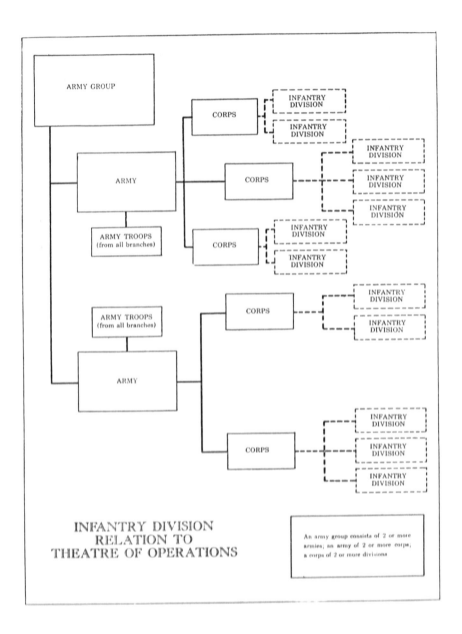

INFANTRY DIVISION
RELATION TO
THEATRE OF OPERATIONS

An army group consists of 2 or more armies; an army of 2 or more corps; a corps of 2 or more divisions

heavy weapon—or base of fire—the Browning automatic rifle.

But an infantry division is much, much more than a bunch of riflemen moving forward with somebody throwing helpful shells over their heads as they advance. A division is a completely self-sustaining unit. It is the smallest complete combination of the ground arms and services. It contains, in addition to its three regimental combat teams, a battalion of medium field artillery, engineer and medical battalions, a cavalry reconnaissance troop, headquarters, signal, quartermaster, and ordnance light maintenance companies, a military police platoon, chaplains, and a band. In combat, this varied group of different units is usually augmented by attached tanks, tank destroyers, antiaircraft artillery, hospitals, and a number of special detachments. A division has planes (for spotting artillery targets and hits), boats (for crossing streams), and hundreds of vehicles ranging from quarter-ton jeeps to a six-ton prime-mover wrecker. It has its own post office, its own post exchanges, more often than not its own newspaper, its own alumni associations, and its own tall tales. All of its many units, however, form a single team for combat.

The infantry division has the primary offensive mission of closing with the enemy's land armies and destroying or capturing them. Defensively, its job is to hang onto the ground it is on, deny it to the enemy, and beat off counterattacks. The division can fight for long stretches without relief (there are several instances of outfits having stayed in the line for more than 100 days without rest), can act independently or can readily serve as part of a larger force, such as a corps or army.

The infantry division has a little more than 14,000 men regularly assigned to it, and is exceeded in size only by the mountain division (a special type of infantry division), which has a few more people and, in prominent addition, more than 6,000 horses and mules. There is a corresponding decrease in vehicles. Mountain troops are specially trained to fight on peaks and slopes, and are astonished if they ever get a chance to march on level ground.

The infantry division, like any military organization, is a coordinated team, and the main function of all members of the team is to get the riflemen in the division forward. The armored division is slightly smaller in manpower (10,000), and is composed of two combat commands and a reserve command rather than three regiments, with 272 tanks as its main striking power. The essential difference between an infantry division and an armored division is that in the first the artillery and attached tank components support the infantry, and in the second the artillery and infantry components support the armor except when the armor cannot lead the way and the infantry must, as happened a number of times in the course of the war.

The armored division is a useful weapon in areas where its mobility and fire power are particularly applicable. As a result, not one of our armored divisions was employed in the Pacific, though smaller tank units proved effective in helping to rout Japs out of their caves and tunnels. An armored division is especially handy during fighting when our forces and the enemy's are moving rapidly—in harassing the enemy's rear positions after a breakthrough, in speeding forward and by-passing strongholds to disrupt enemy communications and supply lines and seize critical terrain features. In general, during large-scale attacks against strong enemy forces, infantry divisions created the opportunity for armor to be used and then the speedier armored divisions exploited that opportunity.

The airborne division is the smallest (8,000 men) and most swiftly transportable of all our divisions, and its main fighting units are infantry. Once it gets into action, however, it is less mobile than an armored division. Paratroops and glider troops are notable for their speed of advance, of course, but this celerity exists only up to getting into combat. Once they reach the battlefield, they have far fewer vehicles than any other division. Airborne units are not ordinarily kept in the lines for long periods, though on occasion they have fought for long stretches (the 82nd and 101st both spent many weeks battling as regular foot soldiers). Their special job is to drop behind enemy lines, capture or destroy such vital installations as airfields or supply dumps, create diversions, delay retreats, and take areas—such as islands—not easily accessible to forces moving overland.

Cavalry divisions—of which our war Army had only one, the famous 1st—have no horses in them. The 1st Cavalry Division is a completely mechanized outfit, and speed has been its hallmark despite the fact that during its early operations, in the Admiralty Islands, it had to dispense with its vehicles and fight dismounted.

No division, no matter what kind, is greater than the men who make it up. The short histories that follow are histories of units, to be sure, but they are the histories, too, of the hundreds of thousands of foot soldiers to whom a casually named town in a foreign land may have been a week of agony, to whom an obscure river or mountain may be a landmark memorable above all others, and for whom no written words will ever catch the import of the moments those names bring back. There are many men who have worn the divisional insignia that are so peculiarly the mark of the fighting soldier. Some of these men served with a division only briefly, and some for months or years. Whoever they are, and wherever they are, they will always be a part of the divisions with which they have fought, for they gave life and blood to our nation's finest combat outfits.

FIGHTING DIVISIONS

1st Infantry Division

THE OLDEST and probably the best known of all American infantry divisions is the 1st, sometimes nicknamed the "Fighting First," often called by its proud members simply "The First," and most recently known as "The Red One." Germans who had seen the red "1" on 1st Division shoulders in North Africa, Sicily, and all over the European continent gave the Division that name, and the 1st's soldiers have since used it themselves. A German, incidentally, involuntarily provided the 1st with its shoulder patch. According to legend, the original red "1" was improvised from the cap of an enemy soldier who had been killed by a 1st Division Doughboy during World War I, when the Division earned the right to proclaim itself first in France, first to fire on the enemy, first to suffer casualties, first to take prisoners, first to stage a major offensive, first to enter Germany and—as an equally notable exception—last to come home.

The Fighting First got off to an early start in this war when, after amphibious training in the States and in England, it surged ashore at Oran on D-day of the North African invasion, November 8, 1942. It fought through Tunisia, taking heavy casualties at Kasserine Pass, but holding its ground against the enemy and living up to its motto, "No mission too difficult; no sacrifice too great," as it hammered away at the vaunted Afrika Korps at Gafsa, El Guettar, Tebessa, and other battlefields.

The 1st's second D-day was at Gela, Sicily. In 37 days, the Division took 18 cities, inching its way up cliffs and along tor-

1

tuous mountain trails, and distinguishing itself by smashing the Hermann Goering Division and taking the important objective of Troina, where the 16th Infantry Regiment, which dates back to 1798, made a gallant frontal attack coordinated with a flank assault by the 18th Infantry, a comparatively new outfit dating back only to 1812.

After Sicily, the 1st sailed back to England to get ready for the invasion of the Continent. On D-day in Normandy, June 6, 1944, it went ashore at Omaha Beach, the most strongly fortified section of the coast. Some of its units suffered 30 per cent casualties in the first bloody hour of fighting, but the Division hung on to the beachhead, forced its way inland by sheer determination, destroyed a whole German division that stood in its way, and prompted Ernie Pyle to write, later, "Now that it is over it seems to me a pure miracle that we ever took the beach at all." For their heroism at Omaha, 740 men of a single battalion of the 16th Infantry were awarded the Bronze Star.

In the July breakthrough out of Normandy at St. Lô, the 1st swung to the west, took Marigny, and then trapped 30,000 Germans near Coutances. In August it moved 300 miles in a week to take Soissons, where in the last war the 1st had suffered 9,000 casualties in four days. (Major General Clarence R. Huebner, who led the Division at the time, had been a battalion commander in the 1st at Soissons in 1918.) The Division continued to Aachen, fighting through the city street by street and house by house after the besieged defenders refused to surrender. Then the 1st found itself in the thick of the Hürtgen Forest fighting. Companies E and F of the 26th Infantry Regiment were completely wiped out, but replacements for the lost units, fighting from foxholes against a heavy tank-infantry attack, avenged their comrades by killing 1,200 Germans in three days. During Rundstedt's counteroffensive in the Ardennes, the 1st successfully attacked in the St. Vith–Malmédy sector, drove on to the Rhine, and, when the 9th Armored Division captured intact the bridge at Remagen, swept across and raced deep into Germany. By V-E Day, all three regiments of the Division had been cited and several smaller units had earned additional honors. The men who wore the Red One had good cause for thinking that the 1st was still first.

2nd Infantry Division

LIKE THE "Fighting First," the 2nd Infantry Division had an outstanding record during the last war, and it became the only division all of whose wartime units were authorized to wear the fourragère of the Croix de Guerre. At Château-Thierry and Belleau Wood, the 2nd —"Second to None," according to its own slogan—made military history a generation ago. Composed then of both Infantrymen and Marine elements, it earned more decorations than any other World War I unit. And among its men was one since-forgotten truck driver who painstakingly adorned the side of his vehicle with a handsome shield framing an Indian head—the Indian Head that thousands of "Second to None" soldiers now wear on their shoulders today.

The 2nd hasn't had exactly a back seat in this war, either. In October 1943, the Indian Head outfit sailed for England, and on June 7, 1944—D-day plus 1—it landed at St. Laurent-sur-Mer in Normandy, while enemy shells were still pouring into the thinly held beachhead. For 70 straight days the Division fought against crack enemy forces, including the formidable 3rd Parachute Division, which the Indian Head men first encountered on June 11 in the Berigny–St. Georges-d'Elle–Ivon sector, and against which the 2nd waged a personal grudge fight for many weeks. The 2nd was instrumental in the fighting around St. Lô that led to the breakthrough out of Normandy, and was credited by Lieutenant General Leonard T. Gerow, then its corps

3

commander, with having been largely responsible for victory in the grim battle of the hedgerows.

Sweeping 300 miles from Normandy to Brittany, the 2nd next set its sights on the besieged German defenders of the port of Brest—among them the same 3d Parachute Division. With the 8th and 29th Infantry Divisions, the 2nd took Brest in 39 days, although military experts had predicted a 90-day campaign.

Next stop on the 2nd's fighting itinerary was the Siegfried Line. The Division had advanced through it to a point near St. Vith and was just getting started on an attack when, in mid-December, Rundstedt launched his famous breakthrough. Cooks, clerks, and military police were thrown into the front lines, and the 2nd held its ground in the snow-covered Bülligen area until the Battle of the Bulge was won.

Then the Division began rolling again. It spilled out into Germany in February and March, capturing Monschau and Ahrweiler, among other key cities. By the end of April, the Division had moved on to Czechoslovakia and had firmly imprinted its name on the historical records of the city of Pilsen, up to then known merely for its beer.

During its last four months of fighting, the Indian Head Division operated under the First Army, and no one was better qualified to judge its effectiveness than General Courtney H. Hodges, the army commander. "What the 2nd Division has done," the general said shortly after the Ardennes fighting, "will live forever in the pages of history of the United States Army."

3d Infantry Division

"TAKE A LOOK at the record, buddy."

That's the answer a soldier of any other division gets when he challenges the claim of 3d Infantry Division Doughboys that their outfit—"The Fighting Third"—is the best in the Army.

The 3d has a superlative record, not only in this war but in World War I, when it earned the nickname "Rock of the Marne" because of its impregnable stand against the Germans' last great counteroffensive. Its participation in three major battles in 1918 is symbolized by the three diagonal stripes of its shoulder patch.

The "Fighting Third" is the only American division which fought the Nazis on every front in this war—North Africa, Sicily, Italy, France, and Germany. It has had more casualties—nearly 35,000—than any other division, and it holds the record for high combat citations, no fewer than 32 of its officers and men having won the Medal of Honor.

The 3d's first D-day came on November 8, 1942, when it spearheaded the landing near Casablanca and, in three days of sharp fighting, took a good slice of French Morocco and was in position to storm Casablanca when the French surrendered. In the final stages of the Tunisian campaign the Division was moved across Algeria by truck and was about to go back into action when the Afrika Korps was knocked out for good.

After two months of training, the 3d went ashore on D-day of the Sicilian campaign. The Division's capture of Palermo was sensational. The Doughboys moved so swiftly that when American tanks and armored cars raced in to take the city, they found it already occupied by the footsloggers. And when the last enemy stronghold on Sicily—Messina—fell to the Allies, it too was taken by the 3d.

At Salerno, the Fighting Third took over the beachhead and pushed the Germans northward and broke through the defenses of Acerno, enabling the British to enter Naples. The Division punched ahead and participated in the bloody crossing of the Volturno.

When the Anzio campaign was launched the 3d again drew "the short straw." Its Doughs splashed ashore in the first wave at Anzio, and for the next four months held on to its toehold in the face of the most furious counterattacks of the war. It was here that the 3d established the record for the most casualties suffered in any one day by an American division.

In the big May push the 3d figured prominently in the liberation of Rome. With only a few days of rest the men started training for their next operation—the invasion of southern France.

Led by Major General John Wilson ("Iron Mike") O'Daniel, the 3d took more than 1,000 prisoners in its first twenty-four hours on French soil, and began a race that carried to Avignon and the Rhône River, then toward the Allied armies which had broken out of Normandy.

The fortress city of Besançon fell in two days, but during October the Division advanced slowly and bloodily in front of the Vosges Line. In November the breaching of the line was completed, and the Doughs moved into Strasbourg.

For its superb fighting on the northern perimeter of the Colmar bridgehead, when it battled through snow, storms, enemy-infested marshes and woods, and over flat plains crisscrossed by unfordable streams, the entire Division was cited by the President. Then, as a major unit of the Seventh Army, the 3d Division drove across the Rhine and deep into Germany. The 3d played a major role in the fight for Nürnberg, and were the first American troops in Augsburg, Munich, and Berchtesgaden.

On V-E Day the "Fighting Third" was at Salzburg, and was using as a messhall the dining room of Schloss Klessheim, where Hitler once housed his more important guests.

4th Infantry Division

WHEN THE 4th Infantry Division sailed proudly past the Statue of Liberty in July 1945, it brought with it two war souvenirs for the people of New York from the people of Paris—a section of the iron gate that bounds the Tuileries Gardens, and a scarred stone cornice from the Hotel Crillon. It was highly appropriate that the "Famous Fourth" should have been selected to bear these gifts, because, when the Parisians, crouching behind the Tuileries gate waited for the liberation of their city, it was the men of the Ivy Division who streamed in and crushed the last German resistance.

Of the Parisians who thrilled at the sight of the shoulder insignia of the 4th, probably very few guessed why its soldiers wore that particular kind of green foliage. The selection of that design is one of the few known instances of authorized military frivolity. "I-vy" is simply the spelling out, in letter form, of the Roman numerals for "four."

There was nothing frivolous about the 4th when it returned to France in 1944 for its second war service in that country. On D-day, the 8th Infantry, one of the three venerable Army regiments that form the backbone of the 4th, surged ashore at Utah Beach and earned the distinction of being the first unit among all the invasion forces to touch the coast of Normandy. For the previous five months, the whole Division, based at Devon in England, had been diligently practicing landings on replicas of the Normandy beaches. Three unit citations were given to elements of the 4th for their work in Normandy, but to offset these honors the division lost its assistant commander, who was posthumously awarded the Medal of Honor—Brigadier General Theodore Roosevelt, Jr.

After the 4th landed, its next accomplishment was to effect the relief of isolated units of the 82d Airborne Division who had parachuted into France and had been cut off for thirty-six hours at Ste.-Mère-Eglise. The 4th helped free Cherbourg, swung back to St. Lô—when it spearheaded the breakthrough by riding through the enemy lines clinging to tanks of the 2nd Armored Division, and smashed toward Paris in the Third Army's drive across France.

By early September, the Ivy soldiers had fought their way into Belgium, and soon cracked the Siegfried Line. A patrol of the 4th's 22nd Infantry Regiment became one of the first American units to enter Germany when it slipped across the border on September 11. During the next couple of months, the division inched its way deeper into Germany, finding itself in December deep in the Hürtgen Forest, where, amid overhead shell bursts, the Doughboys fought savagely against fanatical resistance and one regiment destroyed five German regiments in a 19-day battle.

In the Battle of the Bulge, the 4th held the line in Luxembourg, where its tenacity prompted General Patton to announce, "No American division in France has excelled the magnificent record of the 4th Infantry Division." In January the Ivy Division crossed the Sauer River, and then took one town after another—among them Fuhren, Vianden, Prüm, Adenau, and Reifferscheid. In capturing the last two places, the division moved 20 miles in 24 hours. By V-E Day, it had marched to the Austrian border and was stationed just below Bad Tolz, in Southern Bavaria. It had moved fast, and had hit hard, but, like most of our combat divisions, had had to pay a heavy price for its gains. By V-E Day, the Ivy Division had suffered 21,550 casualties.

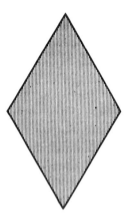

5th Infantry Division

THREE MONTHS before Pearl Harbor, a regimental combat team of the 5th Infantry Division sailed to Iceland. In March 1942 the rest of the division embarked for that island base. By August 1943 the whole division had moved on to England and then Northern Ireland. These early moves were cloaked with secrecy, and little was known of the whereabouts of the soldiers who wore the Red Diamond on their shoulders. By August 1944, however, when the 5th was rushing across France, the Red Diamond was very much in evidence—so much, in fact, that the Germans who had felt its cutting strength decided that the division's nickname was insufficiently descriptive. They gave the 5th a new name—the "Red Devils."

The 5th was no stranger to France, or to German soldiers. In World War I, the Red Diamond Division, entering the lines on June 14, 1918, fought at St.Mihiel and along the Meuse, and took 2,356 prisoners. In this war, it landed in Normandy on July 10, and in two months sped some 700 miles across France to the Moselle River, at one point travelling so fast that it had to halt for five days for its supplies to catch up with it. On its way, it seized Angers, Chartres, Étampes, and other cities, and made forced crossings of 20 rivers, including the Main, Seine, Yonne, Marne, Aisne, and Meuse.

When it reached the Moselle, the 5th was given the mission of establishing a bridgehead on the east bank in preparation for the Third Army's attack on the fortified city of Metz, which had never been captured by a frontal assault although various armies had been trying for a couple of thousand years. On September 8, three years after the first elements of the Division had gone overseas, the Red Diamond Doughboys stormed across the Moselle and dug in on the opposite bank. They held their bridgehead through a nightmare of enemy steel; one unit was counterattacked 36 times during a single 60-hour stretch. With the bridgehead secure, the 5th was withdrawn for a rest, and on November 1st was sent back into the line for the all-out assault on Metz. With the 95th Division on its left and the 80th on its right, and the tanks of the 6th Armored lending support, the 5th attacked on November 9, and ten days later the supposedly impregnable fortress fell to the American divisions.

Ordered to the southern flank of the German bulge during the Ardennes counteroffensive, the 5th saw further bitter action there and helped turn back the enemy threat. Then it went back to its accustomed routine of taking more French cities away from the Germans, helped to clear Luxembourg of the enemy, and, as the war in Europe drew to a close, swung down into Czechoslovakia. On V-E Day, the 5th was at Winterberg.

The Division that had become known along the Western Front for having outrun its supplies achieved a different kind of distinction when it helped drive the Germans out of Verdun and subsequently seized an enemy supply dump. There the Doughboys who had had too little came upon a priceless cache of thousands of German field jackets lined with rabbit fur, and Major General Stafford LeRoy Irwin, their commander, ordered that one be distributed to each Red Diamond soldier. For a while, at least, the Red Diamond men were so snugly dressed that the men of other units sometimes momentarily confused them with our Air Forces.

6th Infantry Division

IN WORLD WAR I the 6th Division was in so many engagements and made so many long marches about France that it was nicknamed "The Sight-Seeing Sixth."

The 6th in World War II did a pretty good job of upholding that reputation. Its six-pointed star shoulder patch has been seen throughout the Pacific, from Hawaii to the far reaches of Japan.

No division had a tougher assignment in the recapture of the Philippines than the 6th. It landed at Lingayen Gulf, Luzon, on D-day, January 9, 1945, and immediately took to the hills in pursuit of the Japs. While most of the other invading divisions were working on fairly flat terrain, the 6th was in the mountains, hacking away at the formidable Nip positions. Not until the Okinawa campaign did American troops get as much artillery as was poured on the 6th from the Japanese mountain guns.

But the 6th kept rolling the enemy from peak to peak. In the first month of the campaign the Sightseers killed 5,000 Japs, and during the fierce battle around Muñoz they knocked out 57 Jap medium and light tanks and destroyed a formidable number of artillery pieces. General Walter Krueger, Commanding General of the Sixth Army, commended the Division for its magnificent performance in this engagement.

Shortly after this battle the 6th's commander, Major General Edwin D. Patrick, was killed by mortar fire while up front with his troops.

The 6th's first mission in this war was the defense of Oahu. The Division reached the Hawaiian Islands in 1943 and relieved the 27th Division of the defensive positions in the southern sector. Later, it took over the defense of the entire island.

In January of 1944 the 6th set sail for Milne Bay, New Guinea, and five months later moved on to the Toem–Wakde area in Dutch New Guinea. In July the Sightseers went into action west of Toem and met and defeated the Japanese in the bloody battle of Lone Tree Hill. This victory was a major one because it secured the Maffin Bay area for the Americans.

With little or no rest, the 6th went into action again. This time the men with the six-pointed star made a landing at Sansapor on the Vogelkop Peninsula in the Netherlands East Indies. Striking swiftly against a surprised Japanese garrison, the 6th rapidly secured the Sansapor coast from Cape Weimak to the Mega River. The Division, in its lightning stroke at Sansapor, captured many prisoners.

The 6th garrisoned this area until late in the year when it joined the vast armada that sailed against Luzon. During the Luzon campaign the men of the 6th established a Pacific record for continuous duty in the line, serving well over a hundred days before being relieved and given a rest at a back area.

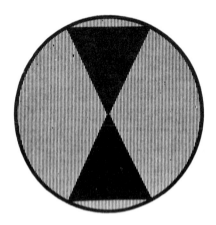

7th Infantry Division

FOR THE MEN of the 7th Infantry Division there is no such thing as unseasonable weather for Jap killing. They have slain the Nips in the sub-zero cold of the Arctic regions, and they chopped them down when it was hitting 125 in the shade of palm trees. After the war was over, they went on to police them in Korea.

From Attu's bleak wastes to the lush jungles of the Pacific the men of the "Hourglass" Division have ranged in search of the enemy, and in doing so have earned two major honors.

At Attu the 7th gained the distinction of recapturing the first American soil taken by the Japanese. And at Kwajalein in the Marshall Islands the 7th, with the 4th Marines, won the honor of first wresting from the Japanese ground he held prior to Pearl Harbor.

The 7th, which was activated in 1940 under the command of then Major General Joseph W. Stilwell, started its battle against the Nips in May 1943, when its men hit the beaches of Attu. For three weeks, in weather that would have broken the spirit of many an Arctic explorer, the 7th was in bitter combat with the enemy. The battle spread into the mountains and into the valleys, and it was not until May 30, when the Japanese threw their all into a fanatical banzai attack that failed, was the battle for the Aleutian stronghold ended.

Three months later elements of the 7th assaulted Kiska only to find that the enemy had fled a few days earlier.

The Hourglass boys shipped from the Aleutians to Hawaii, where they underwent months of rigorous training in preparation for their try at jungle fighting. Early in 1944, the 7th swarmed ashore at Kwajalein, in the heart of the Jap-held Marshall Islands. Six days later the Stars and Stripes was flying over the atoll—and the Japs had lost their first territory of the war.

It was on Leyte that the men of the 7th really started killing Japs. On D-day, October 20, the Hourglassers hit the sand near the town of Dulag and found themselves opposed by one of the crack Japanese divisions—the 16th, perpetrators of the "Bataan Death March." Fighting for every foot, the 7th drove inland, and within four days had captured Dulag, its important airstrip, the San Pablo airfield, and the city of Burauen. Swinging north, the Hourglassers plowed through the rice paddies, waist-deep mud, and monsoon gales to crush Jap resistance and overrun Jap defenses at the key town of Dagami.

But MacArthur gave them little rest. He turned the Division south and told them to eliminate all the enemy from the Leyte watershed as far south as Abuyog. This mission was accomplished under the most adverse weather conditions. The men were pelted by torrential rains, blown down by winds of typhoon velocity, and had to fight flash floods and swollen rivers and streams.

The 7th finished its chore in the Leyte campaign by landing on the Camotes Islands and exterminating all the Japanese on this group. The 7th moved 105 miles on Leyte, covered 1,950 miles in reconnaissance, and killed 16,559 of the enemy.

But the toughest fight for the 7th was yet to come. On Easter Sunday the men of the Hourglass patch landed on the west coast of Okinawa and started a drive across the island. There they met the most intense artillery fire of the Pacific war, and the most stubborn enemy defense. One of the bloodiest battles of the war saw the 7th assault Hill 178 for six days before taking this anchor position in the defense line. When Okinawa was conquered and General Stilwell came to assume command of the Tenth Army, he found his old division—the 7th—waiting for him with a combat record unsurpassed by any fighting unit in the Pacific.

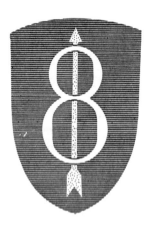

8th Infantry Division

On September 18, 1944, several German pockets on the coast of Brittany were just about liquidated. On that day a German lieutenant general who had managed to sneak from Brest to the Crozon peninsula prudently decided to surrender to the 8th Infantry Division. He was brought before Brigadier General Charles D. W. Canham, assistant commander of the 8th, who stood waiting with a group of armed Infantrymen behind him. The haughty German looked at General Canham and said, "Where are your credentials?" General Canham motioned to his grim-faced Doughboys. "These are my credentials," he said.

That phrase is now part of the permanent history of the "Golden Arrow" Division, formerly known as the "Pathfinder." Its three Infantry regiments are among the Army's best known. The 13th was activated in 1798, the 121st stems from a famous Georgia outfit (and fought against the 13th in the Civil War), and the 28th was the first American combat unit ever to set foot in France when, serving with the 1st Infantry Division in the last war, it landed at St. Nazaire in June 1917.

When the Japs struck at Pearl Harbor, the 8th, a Regular Army division, was immediately assigned to patrolling the east coast from North Carolina to the Florida Keys. It sailed for Europe in December 1943, and trained with the British near Belfast in Northern Ireland. Landing in Normandy on the Fourth of July, it went into action four days later and, during the next ten months, was responsible for the capture of 316,000 enemy prisoners, 250,000 of whom were seized when the Division made a swift dash to the Elbe River in April, establishing a bridgehead there and joining up with the Russian forces advancing west along the Baltic.

The 8th Division's first action was at the Ay River in Normandy. It moved on to capture Rennes, and from there proceeded to the siege of Brest, remaining close to the west coast of France until late in September. During this period the 3d Battalion of the 121st Infantry, while temporarily attached to the 83d Division, made a heroic stand near Dinard, where, on August 9, it was completely isolated for three days, but held out against fierce enemy attacks and saved its wounded by administering plasma dropped by two Cub artillery planes. During August and September, the Golden Arrow Division took 15,000 prisoners.

Turning back toward the east, the division moved into the Luxembourg zone of action, fought in the Hürtgen Forest, and pushed its way across the Roer River backed by a heavy concentration of fire from its own artillery battalions, which one group of Germans reported to be more devastating in their fire than anything they had experienced on the Russian front. The Golden Arrow's big guns poured in a 45-minute barrage of shells on the city of Düren that virtually flattened the place. The 8th went on to cross the Ruhr and the Erft Canal, fought its way to Cologne, stormed the Elbe, and, as the war in Europe ended, was deep in Germany at Schweren. During its ten months of operations in Europe, the Division was out of combat for just ten days.

9th Infantry Division

Stars and Stripes, which ought to know, called it "The Varsity." A newspaper editorial at home dubbed it "Hitler's Nemesis." Nobody knows what Hitler called it, but his term probably wasn't affectionate.

The 9th Infantry Division has a record few outfits can surpass. Its 22,724 casualties attest to the tough fighting it saw. The 17 generals who have graduated from its ranks since its activation (including its first commander, General Jacob L. Devers, now chief of all the Army Ground Forces) attest to its leadership. And the battles it has won attest to its high combat effectiveness.

Port Lyautey, Algiers, El Guettar, Bizerte, Randazzo, Quinnéville, Cherbourg, the Falaise Gap, Remagen, the Ruhr Pocket, the Harz Mountains—these are only a few of the major scenes of action for the veteran 9th.

The red-white-and-blue octofoil—the fifteenth century heraldic symbol for the ninth son—has been borne through Algeria, Tunisia, French Morocco, Sicily, England, France, Belgium, Holland, Germany, and Norway—and the men who now wear it are on permanent occupation duty in Germany.

Their long trip to victory began on November 8, 1942, when elements of the 9th Division, as parts of two separate task forces, stormed ashore at Algiers, and at Port Lyautey and Sojro. For a while two of the 9th's regimental combat teams guarded the

17

Spanish Moroccan border, and were reviewed by President Roosevelt at the time of the Casablanca Conference.

In Tunisia, during the winter and early spring of 1943, the 9th made a 900-mile forced march to Kasserine and fought at Sened and Maknassy, and on May 7, tank destroyers attached to the Division were the first Allied troops into Bizerte, last German stronghold in Africa. Moving on into Sicily, the 9th landed at Palermo and added the key city of Randazzo to its growing list of conquests.

The 9th left Sicily on November 8, 1943, first anniversary of its African invasion. It sailed to England to train for the invasion of France, and landed in Normandy on D-day plus 4. Spearheaded by the 39th Infantry, with its now famous slogan of "Anything, Anywhere, Any Time, Bar Nothing," the 9th Division marched to Quinnéville, pushed on to Barneville, cut the Cotentin Peninsula, and moved on to Cherbourg, where it captured the German commander of the seaport garrison. It was one of the divisions that led the breakthrough out of St.Lô, it fought at Château-Thierry and, on September 2, it began the liberation of Belgium.

By September 5, the 9th had crossed the Meuse River, near Dinant, and eight days later it had entered Germany, south of Rötgen. It fought its way through Saarlautern, street by street and house by house, and as the winter snows covered the battlefield, it battled south of Aachen.

In February, the 9th relieved the 99th at Monschau, moved northeast, and took Einruhr, two miles from the vital Roer River dam, followed by Wascheid and Gemünd. It helped the 1st Division mop up at Bonn, and, late in March, was one of the first outfits to battle at the Remagen bridgehead. A month later, it cut the Cologne-Frankfurt highway, captured the ancient walled city of Zülpich (Clovis had laid siege to it as far back as A.D. 496), and took on the job of reducing the Ruhr Pocket. Not only did the 9th keep the Germans from breaking out of there, but at Schmallenberg, Hitler's Nemeses captured themselves a fine German footwear factory and were issued an unprecedentedly large number of new shoes.

Except for the 47th Infantry, which was detached at the end of the war to travel briefly to Norway, the rest of the 9th spent

18

the closing days of the struggle cleaning up that pocket. The Division took Mechede and Siedlinghausen, and liberated 900 slave laborers from five countries imprisoned at Sinn, on the Dill River.

Ernie Pyle once said, "The 9th is good." He knew what he was talking about.

10th Mountain Division

WHEN THE all-out drive to clear the German forces from Italy began early in 1945, Lieutenant General Lucian K. Truscott, commanding general of the Fifth Army, chose as the spearhead of that push the 10th Mountain Division. It was the sort of break the men of the Army's only mountain division had been waiting for, and their method of waging warfare on the rugged Italian heights more than justified the General's faith in them.

The 10th had been in Italy less than a month before it was in the line in one of the toughest sectors of the Fifth Army front. It was given the task of dislodging the crack German mountain troops from the heights of Mount Belvedere. It was country which a St. Bernard would think twice before traversing, but it didn't bother the hardy men of the 10th, who call themselves the "Mountaineers." For years they had trained in sub-zero weather, and they were chiefly men who had been battling the elements all their lives. The Doughboys who fought through the snowy passes and over the gale-swept peaks were famous American skiers, climbers, forest rangers, park and wild-life service men.

After chasing the Germans from the grim heights of Belvedere, the Mountaineers of the 10th—an admiring high commander called them the "Cat's Whiskers"—piled on the pressure and broke through the stubborn German defense lines in the Apennine Mountains near Bologna. Fighting in the clouds, the 10th is credited with having cleared the last of the mountain

20

barriers in Italy and paved the way for armored elements of the Fifth Army to chase the Germans northward in the Po Valley.

In the relatively short time the 10th was in action it established a reputation through the Fifth Army as an outfit which could scale the heights and stay on top. Once the outfit gained a height it held it. Not once did it yield a peak it had secured.

The Division had many individual heroes.

One was Sergeant Torger Tokle, world champion ski jumper, who was killed in action in March 1945. A buddy of his, telling of Tokle's death, said that the ski champ had died "fighting a one-man campaign to repay the Nazis for the hardship and indignities visited on his family and former countrymen." Tokle's family had been caught in Norway by the German invasion.

Another was Colonel William O. Darby, famous organizer of The Rangers, who was killed on May 1, just before the end of hostilities, while serving as assistant commander of the 10th.

The division was activated at Camp Hale, Colorado, July 1943, and at that time was known as the 10th Division (Light). It was not officially designated as the 10th Mountain Division until more than a year later.

Despite the activation date, the Division's origin dates back to small units which had been in training since 1921, during a period when the Army was experimenting with outfits which would be especially trained to fight in the snow and mountainous terrain. These units were usually composed of volunteers from already activated divisions.

During a training period near the Continental Divide, a pilot, bringing in his bomber to a Colorado airport after dark, reported by radio: "No. 15 to Pueblo. No. 15 to Pueblo. Coming in at eight thousand feet. Gliding. Gliding. Gliding." He flipped over the switch to receive, but instead of the control tower he picked up a tired and slightly bored voice with a New England twang. "Sugar Loaf Mountain Patrol to 10th Division Headquarters," the voice said. "Coming in at twelve thousand feet. Coming in at twelve thousand feet. Walking. Walking. Walking."

The shoulder patch of the 10th has a blue background, the outline of a powder keg, and over this crossed bayonets. Above the patch the men wear a tab bearing the word "Mountain."

11th Airborne Division

"Tokyo Rose" was at her untruthful best on her broadcast of December 7, 1944, third anniversary of the sneak attack on Pearl Harbor.

In delighted tones she told of how invincible Japanese paratroopers, the evening before, had dropped on a vital airstrip in Leyte to destroy scores of planes, kill hundreds of Yanks, and capture the airfield.

No one laughed any harder at this broadcast than did the tough hombres of the 11th Airborne Division. They happened to be on hand when the Nips tumbled out in the dusk, and the ensuing battle was the first paratrooper-*versus*-paratrooper battle of the Pacific. It was a wild fight, there in the coconut groves bordering the strip. Every man for himself. But in the morning the area was stippled with dead Japs, and by noon "The Angels," as the 11th troopers are known to their commanding officer, had tracked down and destroyed every Jap who landed.

The Japs brought with them a flag, later seized in the battle, with the message "Exert your utmost for your country" embroidered on it. It was signed by Lieutenant General Kyoji Tominaga, Imperial War Minister. The flag now hangs at West Point.

The 11th landed on Leyte, 40 miles south of the capital city of Tacloban, on November 18, 1944, and the fight on that island is regarded by its officers and men as the toughest of all the

Division's fights. Troopers who later waged bloody battles for Nichols Field and Fort McKinley, and who used bayonets to assault hill positions and rock caves on Luzon, claim that Leyte was the worst.

The men fought everything on Leyte. Inexperience, rain, mud, howling winds, dense jungles, rugged mountains, and a fanatical enemy. But they never took a backward step during the campaign, despite scores of suicidal banzai attacks by the Nips.

In general, the 11th's mission on Leyte was to clear the Ormoc–Burauen supply trail, the Japs' lifeline, and to squeeze the enemy against the 7th, 77th, and 96th Division troops on the north and northwest coasts. They accomplished this, and much of their movement was done at night. For example, when the 511th Parachute Infantry was given the job of pushing through the Anas Pass, the attack was launched in the dead of night. The Japs, sound asleep in their bivouac, apparently secure in their belief that Americans did not attack at night, were wiped out before they could throw together a defense.

"The Angels" killed 5,700 Japs on Leyte by actual count, and no one will ever know how many more were blown to bits by artillery.

The 11th Airborne made a landing on Luzon, 60 road miles from Manila. Half an hour after reaching the beach the 11th had cleaned out the last Jap beachhead defender, and one of its regiments was racing down Highway 17 to Manila. It moved so swiftly that the Japs, who had mined the bridges, didn't have time to blow them. It was not until the troopers reached the foothills of Tageytay Ridge that the fleeing Japs made a stand. From that point on it was tough going. Mountain guns and mortars bracketed the highway. The Japs were looking down the troopers' throats, but they pushed on up the ever-ascending Highway 17.

On February 3 the 511th made its first combat jump—the third parachute combat jump in the Pacific war. The jump brought about the capture of the Ridge, and "The Angels" headed for Manila, 30 miles away. There was a stiff battle at Imus, ten miles from the Manila suburbs. The troopers broke through the Genko Line, and moved toward Nichols Field. The battle for the airstrip was one of the meanest of the Luzon campaign. Pillboxes dotted the installation, protecting all roads leading to the field. Dual-purpose ack-ack guns abounded. From the outer rim of the field's defenses the Japs poured in fire from five-inch naval guns. Following the fall of Nichols Field, the troopers aided in the capture of Fort McKinley.

Of all the 11th's operations on Luzon, the most daring was the hit-and-run raid on the Japanese internment camp at Los Baños, where more than 2,000 American and European nationals were held. In a combined paratroop and amphibious landing, the troopers struck 25 miles behind the enemy lines to overwhelm the Jap garrison. The Americans sustained only one casualty—a slight shoulder wound suffered by a parachutist.

Oh, yes—one other thing about the men whom Tokyo Rose reported "killed" at the Leyte airstrip. Some of them were among the members of the 11th Airborne who, the following August, achieved the honor of being the first American soldiers to set foot on captive Japan, and who proudly formed the guard of honor as General MacArthur arrived to inspect his first occupation headquarters in Yokohama.

13th Airborne Division

THE SHOULDER PATCH of the 13th Airborne Division is a winged unicorn on a blue shield, and it is a happy choice. Tradition associates the unicorn with qualities of courage and strength, and the elements of the 13th which fought in Europe against the Nazis, displayed these qualities in abundance.

In World War I the 13th was an infantry division, and was prepared to sail overseas when the Armistice stopped all troop movements. In World War II the Division was activated at Fort Bragg, North Carolina, and later was transferred to Camp Mackall, North Carolina, The Airborne Center.

Although the 13th was assigned to the First Allied Airborne Army, it was not committed to action in the European conflict. The 517th Parachute Infantry Regiment, however, which was joined to the division overseas, had had previous combat service. Operating as a combat team, the 517th fought in Italy in September 1944, and then in southern France.

In the Ardennes campaign, when the threat of the German breakthrough was at its height, the 517th fought with outstanding valor. The 1st Battalion of this rugged outfit was attached to the 3d Armored Division and went into combat around Soy and Hotten.

The 2nd Battalion, and that part of the 3d Battalion not guarding XVIII Airborne Corps Headquarters, was attached to the 30th Infantry Division. For their action in this bitter campaign the team was commended by the late Major General Maurice Rose, commanding general of the 3d Armored Division.

After V-E Day, the 13th was stationed in France, at Vitry-le-François. Later it returned to the United States and was about to embark for service in the Pacific when the war ended.

17th Airborne Division

No AMERICAN DIVISION ever made a more spectacular or hazardous entrance into combat than did the 17th Airborne.

Comfortably billeted in England one day, 17th troopers were in the battle zone near Reims the next, ready to throw their power against Rundstedt's best in the Battle of the Bulge.

With Rundstedt's troops grinding forward, the Allies needed all men available. Under cover of darkness, and in treacherous flying weather, the 17th boarded transport planes and was flown to the battle zone.

The men who wear the grasping eagle's claws against a black background on their shoulder patch were given a terrific assignment their first time out. They relieved the 11th Armored Division, south of historic Bastogne, and went into the line between the 101st Airborne Division and the 87th Infantry Division.

Their mission was not to hold, but to attack. And attack they did. Scorning a fanatical foe, swirling snow, roadblocks, and thousands of mines, the 17th drove forward. The troopers slashed into Cetturu, and on to Bouitet, Steinbach, and Limerle, cutting vital highways.

By the end of a month of bitter fighting the men of the 17th broke into Germany near the town of Wiltz.

In February the Division was engaged along the Our River, its job being to hold a bridgehead south of Cleveaux, Luxembourg. In a pre-dawn attack it was one of the units which crossed the Luxembourg-German border along a 22-mile front, and pushed into the Siegfried Line. The men forded the Our River just east of Clerf. Fighting alongside the 6th Armored Division, the 17th captured Dasburg and established a supply line across the Our River.

In March came one of the most successful airborne operations of the war, a feat that helped set up the final drive to Berlin and Nazi capitulation. As part of the First Allied Airborne Army, the 17th helped in the crossing of the Rhine just below the Netherlands border. In dropping across the Rhine the division employed 3,000 gliders without the loss of one due to enemy action. The landing of troops in this dramatic thrust by the First Allied Airborne Army began northeast of Wessel, Germany, and the big march was on. Dorsten fell, then Haltern, followed by Dülmen, Appelhausen, and Münster.

24th Infantry Division

THE 24TH DIVISION doesn't forget.

It was on Oahu when the Japs threw their sneak punch at Pearl Harbor, and the men of the Victory Division have been paying back the Nips ever since.

Thus far the 24th has hit the Nips thirteen times—at Hollandia, Biak, Panaon, Leyte, Mindoro, Marinduque, Subic Bay, Fort McKinley, Lubang, Romblon, Simara, Verde, and Corregidor. Now it is in Japan itself.

The 24th started its slaughter of the Japs in April of 1944 when, in what has been called the most brilliantly conceived and executed tactical maneuver of the Pacific war, it landed in New Guinea for the Tanahmerah–Hollandia operation. In four days the Division had wrested the vital Hollandia airdrome from the enemy, and this was accomplished with only 52 battle casualties. By June 6, the Victory men had killed 1,777 Japs and taken 502 prisoners, and had lost a total of only 43 men killed and 70 wounded. Elements of the 24th then went to Biak and aided the 41st Division in capturing Sorido and Boroke airdromes.

But it was on Leyte, where the backbone of the Japanese defense of the Philippines was broken, that the 24th proved itself one of the great fighting outfits of the war. The men came in on Red Beach, and it was an inferno. Jap mountain guns flayed the landing boats. Zekes and Bettys sprayed the beach.

The dunes were raked by enemy mortar, machine-gun and small-arms fire. But the 24th landed and kept moving. The 19th Infantry Regiment drove up vital Hill 522 before the Japs, who had abandoned this commanding bit of ground during the naval bombardment, could reoccupy their positions. The 34th Infantry Regiment pushed straight inland, repulsing counterattack after counterattack.

The 24th bore the brunt of the fighting on Leyte. It fought the Jap at the crossroads, in the villages, in the rice paddies, along the banks of dirty streams, stalked him through the hills, and rooted him out of his dugouts. For 78 consecutive days, a Pacific record at the time, the men of the 24th were in constant combat, and they killed a counted 7,179 Japs.

The 2nd Battalion of the 19th Infantry is known in the Pacific as the "Lost Battalion" of World War II. In a wide flanking movement designed to put a strangle hold on the Japanese "lifeline" road at Ormoc, the 2nd Battalion remained 13 days behind Japanese lines. Cut off from supplies and unable to evacuate its wounded, the battalion held, despite daily banzai attacks by the desperate Japanese.

But there was no rest for the weary after Leyte.

Elements of the 24th were pulled directly from the line and went to Mindoro as part of a task force, while other elements landed and secured Marinduque.

With only a short rest, the fighting 34th Infantry was attached to the 38th Division to spearhead the landing of that outfit above Subic Bay at the tip of Bataan Peninsula. The 34th led this assault all the way to Zig-Zag Pass, that treacherous divide where the Japanese had prepared a main line of defense. The 34th broke through the pass.

One battalion of the 34th was given the honor of making the amphibious assault on Corregidor. It hit the beach on February 16 while the 503d Parachute Infantry landed on Topside. For nine days the men stood up against—and beat back—fanatical Nip attacks.

Later the Victory men were given the job of mopping-up operations on Verde, Lubang, Romblon and Simara Islands. They didn't miss a Jap. The 24th really remembered Pearl Harbor.

25th Infantry Division

No OTHER DIVISION in the history of the United States Army was ever so quickly in combat after it was formed as the 25th, or "Tropic Lightning" Division.

It was but a baby of two months, stationed on Oahu in the Hawaiian Islands, when the Japanese attacked Pearl Harbor.

Activated from elements of the Hawaiian Division's Regular Army troops in October 1941, it was burying its dead on December 7.

All through 1942, the 25th fretted for a chance to gain revenge against the Japanese. The chance came early in 1943 when the men who wear the Spanish red taro leaf, with a lightning flash on it, cleared for Guadalcanal. The infantrymen went ashore on the open beaches west of the Tenaru River. Their mission was to drive inland 14 miles, envelop the Jap south flank, reduce strong enemy positions on Mt. Austen, and seize the corps objective 3,000 yards to the west.

The rough and broken terrain made supply, communication, and evacuation of wounded extremely difficult. Lack of suitable maps was another handicap. And the Japs were there in abundance.

But the "Tropic Lightnings" slashed forward, and by the 15th of January the Japanese were bottled into three main pockets. The 27th Infantry Regiment fought the Japs in the open. The 35th Infantry fought them in the thick jungles of

Mt.Austen. Some of the meanest fighting of the Pacific war was done by the 25th in clearing the stubborn Japs from these pockets. Early in February, the 161st Infantry made a junction with other division units near Cape Esperance, and the Nipponese occupation of Guadalcanal was over.

After five months of training and conditioning on the 'Canal, the 25th joined in the New Georgia fight for the vital Munda airfield. The 161st was the first to reach New Georgia, and so fierce was the opposition, so miserable the weather, that the 161st required nine days to fight its way to its line of departure. By this time the 27th Infantry had joined the battle, and, in a historic 19-day march through the jungles and mud, secured the important harbor of Bairoko. Following these campaigns, the men of the 25th cleaned up Arundel Island, and fought a bloody battle to secure Vella Lavella Island.

The Division, after eleven months in the jungles, was sent to New Zealand for a well deserved rest. From there it went to New Caledonia, where replacement brought it back to strength.

The "Tropic Lightnings" landed on Luzon two days after the initial assault, and went into the line a week later. Attacking between the 6th and 43d Infantry Divisions, they captured Binalonan and cut Highway 8. The Japs counterattacked furiously at Binalonan, but the 25th held, capturing a tremendous ammunition dump.

The 25th fought a savage five-day battle for the town of San Manuel. The Japs had dug in their tanks, and every building was a fortress. The Nip force consisted of the bulk of their 2nd Armored Division. The 25th's brilliant assistant division commander, Brigadier General James Leo Dalton, II, was killed in the battle for San Manuel.

During all this action the 25th was holding the left flank and engaging the might of the Jap armor, while other American units were dashing toward Manila.

In the Luzon fight the 25th knocked out more than 250 Japanese tanks, mostly with infantry assault weapons, and killed more than 6,500 Nips.

26th Infantry Division

On March 20, 1945, one phase of the European War ended and another was ready to begin. When, on that day, the Third and Seventh Armies made a junction 12 miles west of Kaiserslautern, in southwestern Germany, they sealed the fate of some 70,000 Germans trapped in the Saar Palatinate, and virtually eliminated the last enemy resistance west of the Rhine.

The 6th Armored Division represented the Seventh Army in that significant meeting. And the Third Army colors were carried by the "Yankees" of the 26th Division.

There are plenty of soldiers from all over the country, including the deep South, who now proudly wear the "YD" monogram on their shoulders, but the original Yankees were Massachusetts National Guardsmen who went on active duty nearly a year before Pearl Harbor.

In World War I, the 26th led all other Guard divisions in numbers of combat decorations, but in World War II the Division thought for a while that it might not earn any at all. It wasn't until after nearly four years of training that the Yankees had a chance to play for keeps.

On September 29, 1944, the 26th went into action on the Third Army front southeast of Verdun, taking up positions between the Meuse and the Moselle Rivers. Within a month, the outfit had seen plenty of action east of St.Mihiel, near

Nancy, and north of the Forêt de Parroy. Till early November, however, the 26th had primarily defensive missions.

But on November 8th came the order the Yankees had been waiting for—"Attack!" The Third Army set out to reduce the fortress of Metz. The 26th didn't go after that city. Instead, operating on the southern flank of the assault forces, it advanced 50 miles in a month, crossing the Seille and Saar Rivers, pushing through rugged enemy resistance, and fighting under weather conditions so adverse that its supporting armor and other forces couldn't maneuver effectively, compelling the 26th's Infantrymen to fight on their own.

They did well, taking Morville, by-passing Dieuze to go after Sarreguemines, and, on December 12, plunged into Germany itself at the Blies River.

On December 14, the Division returned to Metz, and a few days later rushed to the aid of the First Army in the Ardennes sector. On Christmas Day, the 26th celebrated its arrival at the scene of trouble by launching an attack on the south side of the German salient extending into Belgium. Many units in that area were trying desperately to break through the German lines and relieve the 101st Airborne, making its stand at Bastogne. One of the first outfits to reach the beleaguered forces was the 26th. Santa Claus himself couldn't have been better received.

27th Infantry Division

Before Pearl Harbor, the 27th Division was commonly known as the "Empire" or "New York" Division, having been composed originally of National Guardsmen from the Empire State. But within a few months of the Japs' attack in Hawaii, the 27th began to travel, and it moved so much during the next three years that now many of its soldiers call themselves "The Galla Vanters." Some liked the name "Tokyo Express," too, and lived up to it when they were among the first Americans to occupy Japan.

After patrolling the west coast of the United States for a few weeks immediately after war was declared, the 27th sailed for Hawaii and manned defensive positions at Kauai, Maui, and Hawaii while training for action farther to the west.

In November 1943 the Division earned its first battle stars. An invasion convoy steamed into the Gilbert Islands, and, while the 2nd Marine Division stormed into the hell of Tarawa, the 27th's 165th Infantry Regiment, with attached troops from other units, went ashore at nearby Makin. It was a quick fight —three days long—but it took its toll of the Galla Vanters, including the regimental commander of the 165th. This was the outfit that in World War I, as part of the 42nd Division, had earned immortal fame as the Fighting 69th.

World War I affected the modern 27th in one other way, too. The Division's shoulder patch combines a monogram of

"NY" with the stars of the constellation Orion—not because of any nights spent in the field looking at the skies, but because in 1918 the 27th decided to pay permanent tribute to its leader, Major General John F. O'Ryan.

After Makin, the 106th Infantry took the small island of Majuro without opposition, and then on to join in the fighting for Eniwetok, in the Marshall Islands, the following February.

The Division fought as an entire unit for the first time at Saipan. Going in on June 17, 1944, two days after D-day, the 27th, fighting alongside two Marine divisions, found itself up against fanatical Jap garrisons entrenched in caves and concrete fortifications. It was a tough campaign all the way through, but it was toughest on July 7.

"Banzai!"

Shrieking their suicidal battle cry, the Japs poured out of their caves and into the 27th's positions in a nightmare of close-in combat. For forty-eight hours the desperate fighting went on, with battle lines virtually indistinguishable as units of both sides mingled in deadly embrace. Well over 2,000 Japanese corpses were counted when the banzai charge was finally stopped, and there were many tales of individual heroism and initiative among the men of the 27th—like the story of the Medics who, cut off from their normal supply of bandages, improvised dressings out of rifle cleaning materials and captured Japanese flags.

Next stop: Okinawa.

Nowhere in the Pacific had the fighting been worse. Dug in at defensive positions of their own choosing, the Japs resisted as only they can. The 27th fought grimly along Kakazu Ridge—"the area of greatest enemy activity," a corps commander said—and on April 19, after a 3,000-yard advance, took the important Machinato airfield. Before he was killed, Lieutenant General Simon Bolivar Buckner of the Tenth Army said of the 27th, "They have paid heavily and they have shown lots of guts."

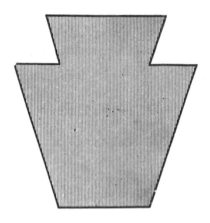

28th Infantry Division

"Roll On" has long been the slogan of Pennsylvania's "Keystone" Division, but for a while in December 1944 it looked as if "Hold On" would be more appropriate. At that time, the 28th, with five months of fighting in France, Belgium, Luxembourg, and Germany already behind it, was deployed along a 25-mile stretch of the Our River, from northeastern Luxembourg to Wallenstein, Germany. And at that time Rundstedt launched the full fury of his counteroffensive against the Keystone's lines. On the first day, five crack German divisions flung themselves over the Our, and within a few days the 28th was single-handedly fighting no less than nine enemy divisions. It held on, though, and one correspondent in the area later called its stand "one of the greatest feats in the history of the American Army."

The 28th, whose nickname is taken from its parent state, had an impressive record in World War I, too. Noted for its fighting in the Meuse–Argonne area, perhaps its greatest single feat was the rescue of the famous Lost Battalion of the 77th Division in the Argonne. Twenty-six years later, the 28th came back to France after having sailed for Europe in October 1943, and having trained in Wales and England for the invasion of the Continent.

The Keystone Division struck its first blow at the enemy on July 22, 1944, shortly after its landing in Normandy. The fury of its assaults on enemy positions led the Germans, who felt that "Keystone" was an inadequately savage description of the 28th's red shoulder patch, to call the division the "Bloody Bucket" outfit. After worming its way laboriously through the hedgerows, the Division broke loose and rolled through France, overrunning Verneuil, Breteuil, Damville, and other cities. It mopped up large numbers of Germans trapped west of the Seine River by the swift Allied advance, and, on August 29 entered Paris, a few days after the city's liberation.

On September 6, the 28th crossed the Meuse, scene of much of its fighting in World War I, went on over the Belgian border, and then fanned out into Luxembourg, averaging 17 miles a day. In mid-September, it became the first division to enter Germany in strength. In November, the 28th cleaned up the Hürtgen Forest, and at the end of the month moved back to the front lines and took up positions along the Our. It was then that it was hit by the Ardennes offensive. Badly battered, the 28th nevertheless kept on fighting determinedly until it was relieved, by which time it had held on so long that the timetable for the enemy breakthrough had been irreparably upset.

After resting and reorganizing, the Division went back to the fight early in 1945. The Keystoners smashed across the Rhine–Rhône Canal and, by February, had taken up positions along the Olef River, near Schleiden. In March, the 28th moved on to the Ahr River, and two months later, as the fight ended, had penetrated into Kaiserslautern.

29th Infantry Division

THE MAJOR had wanted to lead his men into St.Lô, and his men saw that his wish came true. Killed just outside the city while the 29th was battering at its suburbs, the Major had distinguished himself for gallantry in the fierce attack on that key spot. And when, on July 18, the "Blue and Gray" Division finally took St.Lô, its victorious columns included a lone ambulance—containing the flag-draped body of the Major of St.Lô.

The 29th was a veteran division by July 18. For that matter, it was a veteran division on D-plus-1. The day before, June 6, 1944, it had assaulted the German shore positions at Omaha Beach along with the 1st Infantry Division. It had pushed its way inland through minefields and pillboxes and every kind of fortification the Nazis could devise. Its men had loudly answered their own battle cry "29th, Let's go!"

Organized for World War I of National Guardsmen from New Jersey, Delaware, Virginia, Maryland, and the District of Columbia, the 29th had selected as its shoulder patch the blue and gray colors of the rival armies in the Civil War—symbolizing the unity of the formerly embattled states. The colors were combined in a monad, Korean symbol for eternal life. The Blue and Gray Division played a prominent part in World War I, suffering more than 6,000 casualties, and in this war it has more than lived up to that record.

By V-E Day its casualties numbered more than 20,000.

Omaha Beach led to Isigny, and Isigny to St.Lô, and St.Lô to Vire, and Vire to Brest. There the 29th, with the 2nd and 8th Infantry Divisions, laid siege to the German garrison, which finally capitulated on September 18. Swinging east, the Blue and Gray men were ordered to move on the Roer River. They launched an attack northeast of Aachen in November, and, brushing aside enemy defense, had soon taken Siersdorf, Stetterich, Durboslar, and Bettendorf. The stiffest opposition was at the Jülich Sportspalats and at Hasenfeld Gut, but the 29th took both objectives and, by early December, held the west bank of the Roer.

Next objective was the Rhine. The battle-hardened Division set off in February, and in five days had captured 48 occupied places. It swept across the Cologne plain, and fought its way into Jülich, Broich, Immerath, Otzenrath, and Titz.

But these were all smallish places. The 29th had its eye on something bigger. On March 1, it marched victoriously into München–Gladbach, textile center of Germany and up to then the largest German city taken by the Allies. Then the 116th Infantry Regiment, which had been cited for its D-day actions, was assigned to mopping up in the Ruhr area, and the 175th Infantry Regiment, the 1st Battalion of which had been cited at St.Lô, moved into the Klotze Forest. By the war's end, the 29th Division had joined hands with the Russians at the Elbe and was deep in Germany. Later, it was revealed to be part of our Army of Occupation, with its headquarters at the port of Bremen.

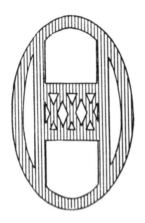

30th Infantry Division

THE 30TH DIVISION got to France a little later than some, but once it started moving it made up for lost time. Joining the Allied assault on the Germans on June 15, 1944, the Division crossed the Vire River and headed for St.Lô, and was soon spearheading the breakthrough out of the hedgerows of Normandy onto the plains of central France. By August 6 the "Old Hickory" Division—nicknamed after the World War I National Guardsmen from the Carolinas, Georgia, and Tennessee, Andrew Jackson's old stamping grounds—had advanced to Mortain and relieved the 1st Infantry Division there.

Everything seemed under control when the Division was suddenly hit by five German armored divisions, hoping to push through to the sea at Avranches and thus split the American First and Third Armies. The brunt of the assault landed on the 1st Battalion of the 117th Infantry Regiment, which threw every available man into the line, stemmed the attack, and was cited for its gallantry. One group of Old Hickory men, cut off for five and a half days, replied to a German surrender demand by saying, "Go to hell! We wouldn't surrender even if our last round of ammo were fired and our last bayonet were broken off in a Boche belly." The Germans never threatened to touch the sea again.

The Old Hickory didn't rest long there. It took Reuilly, crossed the Seine, and by September, had begun an offensive that carried through to Tournai and Brussels and gave it the distinction of being one of the first American divisions to enter Belgium and Holland. Traveling to Belgium, the 30th covered 180 miles in 72 hours. After crossing the Albert Canal and the Meuse, capturing the fortress of Eben Emael, and liberating Maastricht, the 30th got ready to assault the Siegfried Line.

The attack began on October 2. The next day the Old Hickory men, with only their own artillery and basic weapons in support, had broken through the massive fortifications of the line at Palemberg and Rimburg. By October 16 the 30th had made contact with the 1st Infantry Division, crashing the line in another sector, and the two outfits had encircled Aachen. The 30th fought on into the defensive crust of Germany, and abandoned its forward movement only when the Rundstedt counteroffensive made it necessary for the Division to swing back to the Malmédy–Stavelot sector of the Ardennes and join the fight there.

The 30th took care of its share of the counterattack so effectively that the Germans, convinced that no run-of-the-mill division could have treated them the way it did, began calling it "Roosevelt's SS Troops."

When the Allies began rolling again, the Old Hickory reverted to its role of pacemaker. It crossed the Roer, raced for the Rhine, was one of the first outfits to break out from the bridgehead there, and helped to bottle up thousands of enemy soldiers in the Ruhr pocket. By the end of the war, it was stationed at Saalfeld, in Germany.

The oval shoulder patch of the 30th has a story behind it. Its original design embodied an "OH" and the Roman numeral "XXX." In 1918, when the 30th smashed the Hindenburg Line and earned 12 out of 78 Medals of Honor and more than half of all British decorations awarded to Americans, the first shipment of manufactured insignia arrived in Europe for the Old Hickory men to wear. A bunch of Doughboys, receiving them with no explanation of the symbolism, sewed them on sideways. After a while the Division got used to that, and for a long time the 30th considered it right to wear its patch wrong. Finally, in World War II, the Old Hickory men turned their patch back up on end.

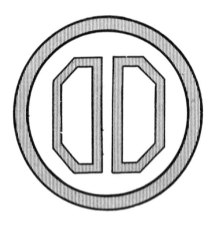

31st Infantry Division

IN UNITY there is strength.

No better example of the truth of this maxim could be found than in the fighting record of the 31st Infantry Division.

The "Dixie" Division originally was composed of men from three "Deep South" states, but when it went into battle in the Pacific there were just as many "damyankees" as "Johnny Rebs" in its ranks. And, when it hit the beaches of Morotai to open the drive that later led to the liberation of the Philippines, its Doughboys were alternately whistling "Dixie" and "Marching Through Georgia."

Forgotten was the War Between the States, and finished were the fist fights over the relative merits of Grant and Lee, Sherman and Stonewall Jackson. The Division had poured it on the Japanese from New Guinea to Mindanao, with a Blue and Gray cooperation that had made it a scourge to the Nips.

The 31st wasted little time overseas before getting into combat. After a brief training period in the bush of Oro Bay, New Guinea, the 31st's fighting regiments moved into action. One combat team, the 124th, went to Aitape, and the other two, the 155th and 167th, to Wakde–Sarmi. The 124th caught a heavy assignment for its first action. In the bloody fighting along the Driniumor River, the 124th killed more than 3,000 of the enemy and played a major part in breaking the back of the by-passed Japanese Eighteenth Army. Fighting was much lighter at

Wakde–Sarmi, but the 155th and 167th accounted for more than 1,000 Japs while on the Maffin Bay perimeter which guarded a Fifth Air Force airstrip.

In September 1944 the Dixie Division sailed from Maffin Bay for the reconquest of Morotai, and on the 15th of the month hit the beaches of this Dutch island, less than 350 miles from the Philippines.

Despite a treacherous landing beach, on which even bulldozers dropped from sight in muck, the Doughs of the Dixie quickly secured a beachhead and by noon of D-day had seized Pitoe Airdrome. Morotai gave our forces control of the Halmahera Sea and cut off 20,000 Jap troops on the island of Halmahera.

For seven months, while Mindanao was by-passed in favor of the Leyte operation, and, later, Luzon, the 31st maintained the perimeter defense for the Thirteenth Air Force. Companies lived on outposts for weeks at a time, supplied by barge and plane; men on the "line" spent their nights on guard in pillboxes; patrols poked continuously into the mountainous jungle in quest of Japs driven to the interior. Several thousand Nips were killed on the island during the seven months, ferreted out by ones, twos, and small forces.

On Mindanao, the 31st expected to fight in the open country, but the Dixiemen found the Sayre Highway no open road. The Doughs fought the Japs in neck-high cogon grass, and in deep forests. The Division's bloodiest fight on Mindanao came when they met the Japs below the Maramag No. 1 airstrip. Here the fanatic Japs had dug in beneath great tree roots. For seven days of close fighting the Americans hacked and dug at the Japs with bazooka, mortar, artillery and small-arms fire. In many instances the Dixies had to root out the Japs with the bayonet.

The 155th Infantry took over the point of the march from Maramag, and scored a rousing rout of the enemy when it surprised an enemy force sunning itself along a stream. In a quick attack the 155th killed 96 Japs while losing but one man.

The Division was commended by Lieutenant General Robert L. Eichelberger, commanding the Eighth Army, for its execution of the operation which split all Jap forces in central Mindanao.

32nd Infantry Division

"Look out! Look out! Here comes the Thirty-second . . ." These are the proud opening words of the "32nd Division March." Not too many people back home know the song, but the strain is familiar to Australian girls, Papuan natives, kids in the Philippines, and to the thousands of soldiers who have seen action under the banner of the "Red Arrow" Division since it began fighting late in 1942 in the evil-smelling swamps of New Guinea.

The fighting reputation of the 32nd is symbolized by its Red Arrow shoulder insignia. On tactical maps the enemy's lines are indicated in red, and the 32nd's patch is a reminder to those who wear it that no enemy has ever stopped the men of the Red Arrow. They have another nickname—"*Les Terribles.*" It was given them by an admiring French general during the last war, when the 32nd earned four battle streamers and was first to crack the Hindenburg Line.

Originally composed of National Guardsmen from Wisconsin and Michigan, the 32nd sailed for the Pacific on April 22, 1942. Landing at Adelaide, South Australia, it trained there, later moved to a camp just outside of Brisbane, Queensland, and was rushed to New Guinea in the fall when Japanese forces crossed the Owen Stanley Mountains, and threatened the vital Allied base of Port Moresby. Many of the Red Arrowmen were flown across the Owen Stanleys—the first large-scale airborne movement of combat Infantrymen in American military history —to take up positions alongside the Australians in the jungles surrounding Jap-held Buna. The 2nd Battalion of the 126th Infantry, however, marched across the Owen Stanleys over an uncharted trail. It took a little over forty minutes to fly across the mountains; to march across them took 49 agonizing days.

The units of the Division that fought at Buna suffered more casualties, many of them from jungle diseases, than their original strength. With the fall of Sanananda on January 22, 1943, the campaign was officially ended, and the victorious Division returned to Australia to lick its wounds and reorganize. Nearly a year later, on January 2, 1944, elements of the 32nd Division went back into action at Saidor, New Guinea, and, in April, at Aitape. Until August, there was bitter fighting against the Japanese Eighteenth Army, trying desperately to get past Aitape and attack the Allied base at Hollandia. The Japs never made it, and had 9,300 men killed in the effort.

From Aitape, part of the Division moved on to Morotai, in the Halmahera Islands, in September, and then the whole Division embarked from Hollandia and headed for the Philippines, landing on Leyte on November 14 and almost immediately going into a fierce 26-day battle in precipitous mountains with deep mud underfoot and tangled forests overhead. In those 36 days the 32nd gained just six and a half miles, but in that slow advance it killed 6,700 more Japs.

Withdrawn from battle on January 4, 1945, the 32d Division rested for three weeks and then moved on to Luzon, plunging into the same kind of jungle fighting and pushing deep into the Cagayan Valley on northern Luzon, where the Japs were making their last stand. When the battle for Luzon ended, the 32nd had to its credit more than 600 days of combat—nearly half the total time the country had been at war up to then.

33d Infantry Division

If the U. S. Army operated on a "finders keepers" policy, the Doughboys of the 33d Infantry Division would be the richest soldiers in the world, with every man a near millionaire.

None of the sourdoughs in the Alaskan Gold Rush struck it as rich as the Doughs of the 33d did in their campaign against the Japs on Luzon in the Philippines. Shortly after going into the line on Luzon the 33d, which is officially known as the "Prairie" Division, earned the unofficial nickname "The Money Division." In attacking the fortified city of Rosario the 33d's artillery scored a direct hit on buried treasure along the highway, hurling prewar silver pesos all over the landscape. The loot, which had been stolen by the Japs and buried as they retreated, was estimated at half a million dollars, and required four trucks to haul it away.

A few days later artillerymen digging new gun positions unearthed $70,000 more in pesos. But it was not until the 33d was battling for Baguio, in the Benguet Mountains, that it really struck it rich. After hard fighting the men of the Prairie recaptured twelve gold mines, including some of the richest in the world. The seven large mines taken by the gold diggers produced 750,000,000 pesos in gold in the year before Pearl Harbor.

June 19, 1945, marked two years of foreign service for the Joes who wear the golden cross on the black circle on their shoulders. The 33d sailed from San Francisco in July 1943, and guarded vital installations in Hawaii until April 1944, when it moved to New Guinea. After participating in the Wakde–Sarmi operation, the Golden Crossers jumped off on Christmas Eve of 1944 for the second Battle of Morotai in the Netherlands East Indies.

The 33d entered the Battle of Luzon on February 10, 1945, relieving the 43d Infantry Division and opening the drive to Baguio, summer capital of Luzon, and headquarters of General Yamashita. The Japs had elected to make their last-ditch stand in and about the mile-high city of Baguio, and the 33d, working with the 32d and 37th Divisions, was in for many bitter battles with the desperate Nips.

For three months the 33d was engaged in savage mountain fighting, over the most rugged terrain of all Luzon. The battles were sharp and severe against an enemy who fought and died on his hilltop positions. There was no easy route to Baguio; it was uphill over the mountains all the way, and the Division had to make its roads as it went. At the beginning of the campaign the 33d had a division front of 20 miles. Three months later, just before the capitulation of the city, the Golden Crossers were fighting on a 65-mile front.

The 33d opened its drive by capturing the key towns of Rosario and Aringay, but to accomplish this it had to wage two vicious battles at Bench Mark and Question Mark hills. The 33d was one of the first divisions in the Pacific to prove to the Japs that they were not the only soldiers capable of successful night attacks. It was in surprise attacks at night that the 33d seized Galiano and Asin which provided the Americans with an all-weather road for the final drive on Baguio.

Several thousand persons, including Brigadier General Manuel Roxas, former aide to General MacArthur, were rescued from the Japs at Baguio, and most of them escaped through the 33d Division lines. Staff Sergeant James Lindquist, of Bloomfield, Connecticut, had the honor of leading General Roxas through the lines. The sergeant, with a carrying party, met the fleeing general on the outskirts of the city, and under the noses of a Japanese outpost patrol. The 33d also liberated Milagros Osmeña, daughter of the President of the Philippines.

34th Infantry Division

WHEN COMPLETE HISTORIES are written of Allied operations in the Mediterranean Theater, the story of the progress of our forces from the coast of North Africa up the long Italian peninsula will be in many ways that of the 34th Division. No outfit has fought harder and longer, and the slow, steady, costly advance of the "Red Bull" Division from November 1942 to May 1945 is a typical example of grim infantry warfare over terrain so rugged that the foot soldier was the only consistently usable means of waging war.

Although its first members in this war were National Guardsmen from Iowa, Minnesota, and the Dakotas, the 34th has a shoulder patch—the background is an *olla,* a Mexican water bottle—inspired by the desert country of the Southwest, where it trained during World War I. It was the first Division to be shipped overseas after Pearl Harbor, its first elements embarking in January 1942, and sailing to Northern Ireland where the 34th trained for the invasion of North Africa. After landing at Algiers, it trained some more for the campaign in Tunisia. Parts of it were badly hit at Faïd Pass, and it had another rough time at Fondouk, but in the famous Battle of Hill 609, the 34th more than repaid the enemy for its previous setbacks and paved the way for the advance on Mateur and Bizerte.

The 34th rested during the Sicilian campaign, and then

sailed for Salerno as a reserve division. Only one 34th unit, the 151st Field Artillery Battalion, got ashore at the start of the invasion, and during eight stormy days it fired more rounds than it had during the whole of Tunisia. One battery of the 151st, its guns overrun by German tanks, withdrew, and then, armed only with rifles, fought back and recaptured its guns.

During the 20 months of fighting in Italy that followed, the 34th's artillery ran its wartime total of shells expended to 1,125,639—the record for any divisional artillery in this war. The 34th, after the whole Division had assembled at Salerno, moved up to the German defense line at the Volturno, and three times bridged that formidable river under fire. Once the assault battalions, after a crossing, had to pick their way single file through a fire-swept enemy minefield. For 76 straight days, the 34th maintained contact with the enemy, finally pushing into the outskirts of Cassino, under withering fire directed by German observers in the Benedictine Abbey at Monte Cassino. On the day the 34th was withdrawn from the city, the Abbey was finally bombed, after ground forces had long been forbidden to assault it. Then five Divisions hammered their way into Cassino, completing the job the 34th had started.

The Red Bull men moved on to the Anzio beachhead, broke out of there on May 25, 1944, marched through Rome, and then took Castellina, Pastina, Fauglia, Leghorn, and other cities, finally bumping into the Gothic Line in October. For four months the Division stayed there, dug in, probing the heavy enemy defenses, constantly patrolling and waiting for an opening. Finally, in February 1945, the Fifth Army launched a heavy attack, and the tired 34th reached Bologna and moved out through the Po Valley as all enemy resistance began to crumble. On May 3, when the German LXXV Corps surrendered in Milan to Major General Charles L. Bolté, commander of the 34th, the Division's long job was done. Fifteen thousand Purple Hearts had gone to wearers of the Red Bull, and more than 3,000 decorations for bravery. The 34th had learned so well the cost of living up to its own motto—"Attack, Attack, Attack!"

35th Infantry Division

WHEN THE 35TH INFANTRY DIVISION was fighting in France in World War I, it had an inconspicuous captain of artillery named Harry S. Truman.

Twenty-seven years later, this same Harry Truman, now President of the United States, stepped ashore at Antwerp on his way to the Potsdam Conference with Churchill and Stalin, and inspected a guard of honor from the 137th Infantry, one of the regiments of his World War I Division, the fighting 35th.

Lining the President's route from Antwerp to Brussels were 1,600 Doughboys from the same regiment, all wearing the same Santa Fé cross on their shoulders that the President wore against the Kaiser's armies.

The President was well guarded. The men of the 35th who lined the streets to honor and protect their commander-in-chief wore five battle stars, and could tell of fighting with five armies in the battle to crush the Nazis.

From the time the Santa Fé Doughs hit Omaha Beach in France in July 1944, until the Germans surrendered to the might of the Allied forces, they served with the American First, Third, Seventh, Ninth and Fifteenth Armies, and fought the Wehrmacht from St.Lô to the Elbe River.

The 35th was in the line two days after hitting Omaha Beach and began battling toward, and finally into, rubble-strewn St.Lô. It fought its way across the Cherbourg peninsula, blasted Vire, and, in one of the most vicious battles in France, repulsed a counterattack that threatened to overrun Avranches. Despite heavy casualties, the Santa Fé men swung east to recapture important terrain near Mortain, and rescue the 30th Division's "Lost Battalion."

Spearheaded by the machines of the 4th Armored Division, the 35th rushed still farther east to take town after town. Once it hit the Le Mans–Orléans highway, it drove to the important stronghold of Orléans and captured it in a night and day of savage battling.

The 35th continued to drive straight across France. It spanned the Loing, Seine, Loire, Marne and Meuse Rivers. In mid-September, still rolling at top speed, it liberated the city of Nancy. For three months the Santa Fé patch boys kept moving forward, and on December 5 fired their first round of ammo into Germany. They swept past Sarreguemines, and then crossed the Saar.

Then Rundstedt launched the Battle of the Bulge.

The Santa Fé then made three great jumps. It was shifted to the First Army and, during the Christmas holidays, plunged into battle. Despite terrific punishment, the 35th repulsed attacks by four crack German divisions and eliminated the threat to the right flank of the Bastogne highway.

This threat ended, the Santa Fé made a dramatic leap to the Seventh Army in the south, where a breakthrough was threatened. Again the 35th held, and was ready for a third and even more sensational jump. In bitter weather it was rushed 292 miles north to join the Ninth Army.

It reached Rheinberg, and was the last of the Ninth Army elements to gain the Rhine. Worn from constant battles, the Santa Fé Doughs banged away at the Germans trapped in the Wesel pocket, and drove into the Ruhr. It met bitter opposition all the way, but it would not be stopped.

Later, the 35th Division joined the Fifteenth Army, and at the war's end had taken more than 20,000 prisoners, and received more than 3,000 awards.

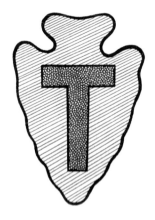

36th Infantry Division

"DEEP IN THE HEART OF TEXAS" is the theme song of the "Texas" Division, but it has been a long time since its men have seen the prairies of the Lone Star State.

The first American Division to land on continental Europe, the Texans have been deep in the heart of Italy, France and Germany since late in 1943.

The rough, tough men who wear the blue arrowhead and green T on their shoulders ended their campaign against the Germans by capturing two of the Nazi chieftains who had done the most to make life miserable for the Division since it first went ashore at Salerno in September 1943. The first to fall into the clutches of the Texans was Field Marshal Von Rundstedt, ace strategist and planner of the mighty winter offensive. Shortly after, the biggest Nazi of them all, Reichsmarschal Hermann Goering, was taken to the rear under cover of the 36th's rifles.

The 36th's baptism of fire was a bloody one. For five days after the Division struck at Salerno the issue was in doubt, and the Texans suffered heavily before the beachhead was secured. But there was to be no rest for them. Few Doughboys in this war have undergone a more merciless fire than did the Westerners in their attempts to cross the Rapido River. Crack German troops raked them with every weapon of warfare when they plunged into the swiftly moving waters of the Rapido.

It was in this campaign, near Altavilla, that the 36th produced one of the outstanding heroes of the war.

A private first class, Charles E. Kelly, voluntarily joined a patrol and located and neutralized enemy gun positions. Again voluntarily, Kelly made his way under intense fire to a hill a mile away, reporting on his return that it was held by the enemy. Joining another patrol, he assisted in putting two machine guns out of action. He found an ammunition dump under enemy fire, and joined in its defense. He protected his position all night and held off an enemy detachment the next day to cover the withdrawal of his outfit. Kelly, now known to all Americans as "Commando," was awarded the Medal of Honor for his heroic action.

Following the savage battle for Cassino, the Texans were given seven weeks of rest and then thrown back into battle. It joined the beachhead forces at Anzio, and by a brilliant maneuver captured Velletri and paved the way for the fall of Rome. The men hoped for a rest in Rome but they didn't get it. They moved through the Eternal City on the double, hot in pursuit of the fleeing Germans.

The Texans made their second landing, in southern France, in August of 1944. Objectives were gained so fast that the Division got into the position east and north of the German Ninth Army at Montélimar and cut it to ribbons. A month after the Division hit the beaches at St. Raphaël, it had gained 300 miles and was in the foothills of the Vosges, facing the formidable Moselle River.

The Moselle was one of the German's heaviest fixed lines of defense, but the Texans outwitted the defenders. Led by the 70-year-old Mayor of Raon-aux-Bois, who knew every ripple of the Moselle near his town, the 1st and 3d Battalions of the 141st Infantry, wading waist deep, sneaked across a little-known ford during the night and established a bridgehead. Recovering from their surprise, the Germans turned murderous fire on the battalions. But the Texans drove on into the forests that covered the slopes of the Vosges. The 442nd Infantry Combat Team, made up of Japanese-Americans, distinguished itself with a savage attack that took the town of Bruyères. Mines, snipers and artillery made the battle in the forests a nightmare.

54

The 36th kept moving, and before it rested had established the modern army record of 132 days of consecutive combat. The Texans took Colmar and Oberhoffen, and smashed on across the Rhine, taking Wissembourg, to plant the Lone Star flag of Texas deep in the heart of Germany.

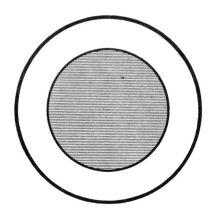

37th Infantry Division

In May 1942, the 37th Division sailed under the Golden Gate.

Today, more than 3,500 "Originals" form the nucleus of Ohio's fighting "Buckeyes" who have conquered the Japanese at New Georgia, Bougainville, and at Manila and Baguio in Luzon.

Few outfits in the Pacific have seen more of the enemy, and killed more of the enemy, than the belting Buckeyes. From the time in 1943 when they drove ashore at New Georgia, until they chased Yamashita and his puppet government from the hills of Baguio, summer capital of the Philippines, almost two years later, the men from Ohio have faced the enemy almost continuously.

Despite the 37th's magnificent spearheading of the drive that liberated Luzon and recaptured Manila, the Buckeyes probably will be best remembered by historians for their slaughter of the Japanese on Bougainville in the Northern Solomons.

The 37th hit Bougainville in November of 1943 as part of a Marine amphibious corps and won its beachhead on Empress Augusta Bay with comparative ease. But three months later the same 40,000 Japanese who had been pushed across the hills struck in full fury, and the bloody second battle of Bougainville was on. The Japanese attack was led by the 6th Division, one of the Imperial Army's best and the Division which perpetrated the rape of Nanking.

Four times the Japanese, backed by concentrated artillery

fire, slashed at the 37th's defense lines. And four times they were hurled back with a loss of 8,000 men. The heaviest fighting was concentrated on Hill 700, the "Hill of Heroes," the 37th calls it. The battle raged here in an area not more than 100 yards long and 50 yards wide. Hill 700 and nearby Hill 260, where some of the most bitter hand-to-hand fighting of the war was fought, are now classrooms for the training of replacements.

On January 9, 1945, the Buckeyes came ashore on D-day at Lingayen Gulf and spearheaded MacArthur's return to Manila, which was reached on February 4. The Doughboys of the 37th walked and fought the full 142 miles from Lingayen to Manila. In the capital of the Philippines the Buckeyes had to forget all about jungle fighting, at which they were masters, and adopt a new kind of warfare—street fighting.

Every building was a fortress, every street corner was a machine-gun nest. Thousands of mines had been sown by the Japanese and booby traps abounded. But the Buckeyes beat the Japs at their own game, and when the city finally fell the 37th had accounted for 12,000 dead Nips.

From Manila and its stifling heat the Buckeyes moved into the mountains in northern Luzon, and in conjunction with the 33d Division liberated the mile-high city of Baguio, anchor of the Japanese northern defense line. It was from Baguio that General Yamashita and President Laurel, puppet head of the Philippines, fled to what Tokyo Rose called a "more central location."

When the news of Germany's surrender came the 37th was too busy to celebrate. It was working in treacherous Balete Pass, the southern gateway to the Cagayan Valley and Luzon's northern coast.

Shortly after, the men of the 37th, who wear as a shoulder patch a red-and-white disc which appears on the state flag of Ohio, broke into the valley and eliminated the thousands of Japanese defenders there.

38th Infantry Division

SOMETHING NEW HAS BEEN ADDED to the insignia of the 38th Infantry Division. Across the top of the shield-shaped red-white-and-blue patch, with its interlocking C and Y, the men who wear it now like to append a scroll with the words "Avengers of Bataan."

It belongs there too, because the Doughboys of the 38th, the Cyclone Division, spearheaded the drive which annihilated the Japanese forces on Bataan in the battle that liberated Luzon.

During this drive, elements of the 38th swept through Balanga, Pilar, and across the neck of land to Bagac—the same route over which the Japanese had tortured and humiliated the heroic American defenders of Bataan in the infamous March of Death in 1942.

The Cyclone Division—it got its name in 1917, at Camp Shelby, Mississippi, when the tent-city area in which it was bivouacked was levelled by tremendous winds—struck like a cyclone when it landed on Luzon in January of 1945. The Cyclones came ashore near Subic Bay on the famed peninsula, where they cut behind the Japs then fighting our Lingayen Gulf forces on the central plains of the island.

In a fierce, 16-day action, during which the Japs threw everything in the book at them, the Cyclones smashed through an intricate maze of fortifications to take Zig Zag Pass, key defense of the Bataan Peninsula. The Japs used all their resources in an effort to hold this pass. Mountain guns blasted the winding road to the pass. Mines made every step a dangerous one. Machine guns swept every twist and turn, and from caves and heavily fortified pillboxes the Nips poured continual fire. But the 38th was not to be denied.

One combat team made an amphibious assault at Mariveles, on the tip of the peninsula, and caught the Japs flat-footed. Another struck swiftly down the east coast to sweep along the Death March route. Other units landed, on D-plus-4, on Corregidor to assist in the defeat of that Jap-held rock fortress.

The Division was then divided up into three regimental combat teams.

One force mopped up remnants of enemy troops on the peninsula. Another, plus a provisional company organized from the division artillery, struck north and west of Zig Zag Pass against powerful enemy defenses in the rugged Zambales Mountain ranges, while the third was charged with the reduction of enemy defenses on the remaining three islands—Caballo, Fort Drum and Carabao—guarding the entrance to Manila Bay. This force, the 151st Infantry, had previously occupied Grande Island, in Subic Bay.

With these missions completed, the Cyclones moved as a unit to the Sierra Madre Mountains northeast of Manila to give battle to Jap forces drawn up behind the Shimbu Line, an area defended by almost impassable terrain in addition to a well developed and interlocking series of caves, pillboxes, tunnels, and artillery emplacements. To break this line, the Doughs of the 38th fought a series of savage battles. The Japs were burned from their caves with flamethrowers, blasted out with satchel charges, and rooted out with bayonet and hand grenades. The engagement came to an end when the 38th seized the Marikina River line and captured Wawa Dam, an important source of water supply to Manila.

When Wawa Dam was seized the Avengers of Bataan had killed 17,600 Japs, captured 466 prisoners, and established an exceedingly low ratio of KIAs to enemy dead—1 to 36.

40th Infantry Division

WHEN MAJOR GENERAL RAPP BRUSH led the veteran 40th Infantry Division into the Philippine liberation campaign, he began retracing the steps of his youth.

On the day the 40th liberated the city of Lingayen, General Brush rode through its shell-pocked streets.

"This doesn't look like much of a playground for a boy," he remarked.

As a boy in Lingayen, where his father was Military District Commander in 1901, the leader of the "Sunburst" Division had taught Filipino youngsters to play baseball. When General Brush had led his Doughboys in a lightning, 10-day liberation of the island of Panay, he established his headquarters in Iloilo, where his father once served as commanding general.

The thorough knowledge of the country owned by General Brush, plus the blazing combat spirit of his men, made the 40th a terror to the Japanese.

The Doughboys of the 40th were better than green hands at fighting when they landed on Luzon on D-day. Early in 1944 they had been in action on New Britain in the Bismarck Archipelago. The Infantrymen, knifing through snarled jungle growth, continued the offensive initiated by the 1st Marine Division. From Talasea on New Britain's north coast, Doughboys of the 40th jumped 25 miles eastward to capture the Cape Moskins airdome, and make escape-proof the trap which surrounded thousands of Japanese troops in the Rabaul area.

The 40th, known also as the "Rattlesnake" Division, struck with the speed of that reptile when it landed at Luzon. By nightfall of D-day, the 40th had rolled on past Lingayen and crossed the Agno-Calmay River. On January 21, 11 days after the invasion, soldiers of the 40th entered Tarlac, provincial capital and key highway-railroad junction. Crossing the Bamban River, Sunburst footsloggers were the first American troops to reach Clark Field, target of the earliest Japanese bombing attack in the Philippines after the outbreak of the Pacific war. The 40th went on to capture Fort Stotsenburg and Camp O'Donnell, where hundreds of prisoners of Bataan and Corregidor died.

At the end of 53 continuous days of fighting on Luzon the 40th had killed 6,145 of the enemy.

Early in March elements of the 40th surprised the Japs by landing on Panay Island in the Visayas. On the third day of fighting, the Doughboys captured Iloilo, second most important city in the Philippines. The city had been badly damaged by the Japanese but the harbor facilities were immediately put to use. Within ten days all of Panay had been liberated, and American planes began landing on airstrips at Santa Barbara and Mundurriao.

Units of the 40th landed on Guimaras and Inampulugan Islands, between Panay and Negros, to erase any threat to American sea lanes in the central Philippines. Late in March the entire Division jumped across Guimaras Strait for an invasion of Negros.

Twenty-seven hours after H-hour the Sunbursters had captured Bacolod, capital of Negros Occidental. By June 1 the 40th had killed and captured nearly 5,000 Japs on Panay and Negros.

While the 160th and 185th Infantry Regiments were operating in the Visayas, the 108th effected a landing on Masbate Island in the Visayan Sea between Luzon and Panay, and destroyed the Jap garrison there. The Doughboys of the hard-hitting 108th then went ashore on the northern coast of Mindanao, to seal the doom of the Japs trapped between the 31st and 40th Divisions.

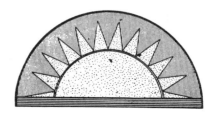

41st Infantry Division

FROM PAPUA'S BLOODY SANANANDA in early 1943, to Zamboanga's matted jungles more than two years later, the 41st Infantry Division established a combat record second to none.

The men who wear a golden setting sun against a crimson background for a shoulder patch call themselves the "Jungleers," and rightly so. The first complete division to reach the Southwest Pacific, they have done more jungle fighting than any other American outfit. So mercilessly have they scourged the Japanese that Tokyo Rose, when she spoke of the 41st, always referred to them as "The Butchers."

The Jungleers reached Melbourne in April 1942, and had their first fight with the Japs, after flying over the Owen Stanleys, at Sanananda that December. Outnumbered, and with little or no naval or air support, the 41st had to rely on scanty supplies brought in by air over the Owen Stanley Mountains, and, when the fighting was finished, they came out in rags.

Six months later the Doughboys of the 41st went ashore below Salamaua for the "Foxhole Furlough." Here they set a theater record—76 days of unrelieved jungle fighting. They presented a strange sight at the end of the campaign, most of them emerging from the bush wearing Japanese naval uniforms. Their own clothes had worn out long before, and only the capture of Jap clothing saved them from fighting in the raw.

In 1944, within 36 days, the 41st broke the grip the Japanese had held on New Guinea for two years. In a series of strides up 900 miles of New Guinea's tangled jungle, the 41st, between April 23 and May 27, smote and conquered the foe at Aitape, Hollandia, Wakde, and Biak. By these brilliant successes, the pathway to the Philippines was cleared.

Many tactics our forces later used against the Nips were developed by the Jungleers in their New Guinea fights. The 41st Division was the first outfit to be opposed by Japanese tanks, and it was on Biak that the Nips first resorted to cave defenses. The 41st's method of breaking up the cave defenses was employed at Saipan, Leyte, and Iwo Jima.

The Jungleers started their work in the Philippines on February 28, 1945, when they landed at Palawan, westernmost isle of the Philippine group. In 34 combat crowded days the Jungleers bettered their 1944 mark of four assault landings in 36 days by making the same number in 34 days. After Palawan, a second punch was delivered in the initial invasion of Mindanao. Elements of the Division then struck Basilan Island, and in three days secured it. On April 2 the 41st, quite at home on beachheads now, landed on the tip of Tawitawi and destroyed the Japanese there.

The 41st, originally composed of National Guardsmen from the Northwest, have a sign "End of the Oregon Trail." They planned all along to plant it in the front yard of the Imperial Palace in Tokyo, and their chance finally arrived as they came victoriously ashore in Japan as part of the Army of Occupation.

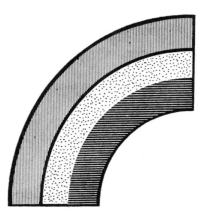

42nd Infantry Division

AMERICA'S BEST KNOWN DIVISION, the 42nd, does not believe in hiding its light under a bushel.

Visitors to torn, battered Germany, report that one can follow the path of the fighting 42nd by keeping an eye out for rainbows painted on the sides of buildings.

Let an element of the Division halt for a moment and some GI, paint brush in hand, would splash the red, gold and blue of the rainbow, for all to see.

The 42nd got its nickname in World War I when one of its majors, noting that its personnel was drawn from 26 states and the District of Columbia, said "This Division will stretch over the land like a rainbow."

The major who inspired the nickname has moved up in grade since that time. He is now General of the Army Douglas MacArthur.

The 42nd was late getting into action against the Nazis, but once in the line, it fought with the same dash which characterized the World War I Rainbow, in the Champagne, Champagne–Marne, and Aisne–Marne offensives.

The Division first faced the Wehrmacht in December 1944, when, under the Seventh Army, it was given the unglamorous role of plugging gaps and weak spots on the army's right flank near Saarbrücken. Near the middle of February the Rainbows were readied for the attack, and it was at this time that the Division was officially announced as part of the Seventh Army.

A month later, the 42nd made its first penetration of Germany. In bitter weather, the men with the rainbows 'round their shoulders, drove through the Hardt Mountains. Early in April the towns of Dahn and Busenberg fell to the slugging Doughs. These conquests were made doubly difficult by the weather and terrain. Vehicles could not be used on the icy mountain roads, and it was necessary to move in supplies by pack mule.

Rolling east of the Rhine, the 42nd took Fürth and Schweinau, drove on to capture Schweinfurt, and then joined in the assault on Nürnberg.

The 42nd was the first division to reach Munich, and from Munich it went on to infamous Dachau, and helped liberate 32,000 inmates of this nightmarish Nazi prison camp.

The Rainbows moved into Austria, collecting prisoners by the thousands. One of the Nazi "prizes" to fall into the Rainbow's hands was Major General Wilhelm, German communications chief.

Following V-E Day, the Rainbow occupied Ritsbah, the Hollywood of Germany.

43d Infantry Division

FROM THE ROCK-BOUND COASTS OF Maine to half the islands in the Pacific and to Japan itself—that is the war record of New England's 43d Division. The veterans of the 43d, drawn from Maine, Rhode Island, Vermont and Connecticut, wear the black grape leaf on a red quatrefoil as a shoulder patch, and are qualified to wear four campaign stars on their Asiatic ribbon.

The "Winged Victory" Division, which was organized shortly after World War I, has many units which date back to the Revolution. Reactivated early in 1941, the New Englanders have been almost constantly on the go ever since.

The 43d's first assignment overseas was a tour of duty in New Zealand, when it appeared likely that the Japanese might invade that country. It then shipped for a brief stay in New Caledonia. Early in 1943 the New Englanders reached Guadalcanal before that campaign had ended and aided in the mopping up of isolated Japanese units.

A month later the New Englanders began the war in earnest. Their first mission as a unit was the invasion of the Russell Islands, and the men with the twang were disappointed when they took the islands without opposition. But they were soon to long for this quiet invasion. With elements of the Army, Navy and Marines, the 43d, in late June of 1943, assaulted New Georgia, landing on Rendova Island.

For 35 days of what many authorities believe to be the

dirtiest, roughest campaign of the early war in the Pacific, the 43d fought for Munda airport. As yet inexperienced in the ways of jungle fighting, the 43d was opposed by some of the crack elements of the Imperial Japanese Army. All the tricks of the jungle which eventually became old stuff to our troops were strange to the men of the 43d in the fight for Munda. They had to learn the hard and bloody way, and they did. On August 5 the 43d broke the Japanese resistance and seized its prime objective—the vital Munda airstrip.

New Guinea's stinking hell was the next stop for the men from the land of the fir and pine. They joined other forces at Aitape and had a share in the bloody battle of the Driniumor River. It was there that the Japanese, in an effort to break through the encircling American forces, were slaughtered by the thousands as they attempted a crossing of the swift-flowing Driniumor.

The 43d drew a mean assignment in the invasion of Luzon. Landing on D-day on January 9, 1945, at Lingayen Gulf, the 43d's mission was to take the left flank and secure the hill masses and road network in order to block off the strong Japanese forces in the mountains at Baguio.

The Japanese defenses of the island were such that the 43d bore the brunt of the fighting in securing positions on Lingayen Gulf. While other assault divisions were moving south over comparatively flat terrain, and over highways, the New Englanders were deep in the hills. There they encountered heavy mountain guns and deep cave positions, and were forced to move their supplies up trailless slopes. For the first 30 days the 43d was in constant battle with the enemy.

Later the 43d moved to the east of Manila and helped clear the Nips from the hills near the city. One of the most brilliant campaigns in the fight for the liberation of Luzon was staged by the 43d when, working with guerrilla forces, it took a mountain dam which was vital to Manila's water supply.

44th Infantry Division

BEFORE PEARL HARBOR, the shoulder patch of the 44th Division was a familiar sight around New York. When it went into training in September 1940, the 44th was composed of National Guard units from New York and New Jersey. The blue-and-orange colors of its patch are those of the Netherlands House of Nassau, which controlled the original settlers of the Division's home areas. After Pearl Harbor, however, the 44th left the East for extensive combat training, and remained on duty at various camps in the United States for four years until September 1944, when it embarked for the European Theater of Operations shortly after the Allied invasion of southern France.

The 44th soon became a part of the Seventh Army, which had conducted those landing operations and was pushing northward for a junction with the forces that had driven into Europe from Normandy. In October, just east of Lunéville, France, the Division went into action and took part in the Seventh Army's drive to secure several passes in the Vosges Mountains. It hadn't been committed to battle long before it learned a severe lesson in what war can be like at its worst.

Six days after its first taste of blood, the 44th was hit by a heavy German counterattack, and its front lines were pierced. The Division rallied and nullified this blow, and then, working with the French 2nd Armored Division, it started a slow, steady advance through Alsace-Lorraine, taking Leintrey, Avricourt, and Sarrebourg. One battalion, accompanying the French, reached the Rhine at Strasbourg. On November 25, while the two Allied divisions crept forward over snow-covered ground every inch of which was savagely defended, one battalion of the 44th won itself a citation for especially distinguished action and, in doing so, saved the whole Division and neighboring forces from rough treatment and possible annihilation.

The 2nd Battalion of the 114th Infantry Regiment, defending a 4,000-yard sector north of Schalbeck, France, that day, was suddenly struck by a picked panzer division, which had the mission of grinding through the 44th, retaking Sarrebourg, and cutting off all the Allies east of the Vosges. Although the Germans had more men and more fire power, the battalion grimly held its positions, fighting against German 88s from shallow foxholes, and prevented the enemy from breaking through. General Patch later credited the battalion with saving the whole Seventh Army.

By December the Division, thoroughly conditioned to combat, had reached the Maginot Line and had taken the massive concrete and steel blockhouses at Fort Simserhof. On New Year's Eve another panzer division hit the 44th near the Saar River, and the 44th inflicted 6,000 casualties on it while turning back 20 vicious enemy attacks. One of the casualties was the first SS Division commander to be captured on the Western Front.

From then on the 44th had comparatively clear sailing. Under the command of Major General William F. Dean, it consolidated its positions below the Saar during January until it was relieved in March after 144 days of combat. In the succeeding months of operations, it rolled deep into Europe as German resistance began to crumble on the southern front, crossing the Rhine, capturing Mannheim, and slashing into the Austrian Tyrol. V-E Day found it firmly established at Imst, Austria, and on that day the 44th made contact with the Fifth Army coming up from Italy.

45th Infantry Division

In May 1943, troops stationed at Camp Patrick Henry in Virginia witnessed one of the strangest spectacles in American military history—a campfire war dance put on by soldiers about to embark for overseas. They were some of the 1,500 American Indians—from 28 tribes—who belonged to the "Thunderbird" Division. Composed in 1940, when it was activated, of National Guardsmen from Oklahoma, Colorado, New Mexico, and Arizona, the 45th was much changed after its first two years of foreign service. Few of the Indians were left in its ranks. Its total casualties had amounted to twice its original strength.

But the 45th was used to changes. For instance, for years its shoulder patch, four-sided for the states to which it owed allegiance, had displayed a respectable old Indian design—the swastika. When the Nazis rose to power, the Division hastily substituted for this unseemly symbol another traditional Indian figure—that of the thunderbird, the Red Men's "sacred bearer of unlimited happiness."

At Oran, the Division trained for the first invasion of Europe —Sicily. On D-day, the 45th stormed ashore at Scoglitti, and in three weeks had overrun 1,000 square miles of enemy-held territory, moving so relentlessly that one German prisoner complained peevishly, "Don't you ever sleep?" The high spot of the 22-day campaign was the fierce fight for "Bloody Ridge," just before the Thunderbirds took San Stefano.

When the Allies landed at Salerno in September, the 45th went in, on D-plus-1, at Paestum, and fought for four bitter months through the Apennines until it was relieved on January 9, 1944. During this stretch, the Division crossed the Volturno River, took Venafro, and battled the enemy on icy mountaintops where it was so cold the Doughboys couldn't dig foxholes in the hard ground. Some of the Thunderbirds turned muleskinners, in order to get supplies to the front lines over trails impassable for vehicles. After a brief rest, the 45th went ashore again at Anzio, and remained there under ceaseless enemy fire for 76 days. It turned back the major German counterattack calculated to drive the Allies back into the sea, and three units of the Division received citations for heroism.

After the breakthrough out of the beachhead, the 45th marched north to Rome, and was relieved again on June 6—D-day in northern France. By the time the Division sailed for its fourth invasion—southern France—it had already completed 271 days in the line. With other units of the Seventh Army, it rolled up the Rhône Valley and into the Vosges Mountains, where it ran into tough enemy opposition. Then it fought its way into the heart of Germany. Under the command of Major General Robert T. Frederick, one of the youngest division commanders in the Army, who was wounded nine times in battle, the veteran Thunderbirds took city after city, including the supposedly by-passed Aschaffenburg, whose fanatical defenders, including young boys and girls, put up some of the bitterest resistance the 45th had ever encountered. The Nazi shrine at Nürnberg and the Nazi hell at Dachau were next, and the 45th climaxed its long months of service by marching triumphantly into Munich. The soldiers who had had to stop wearing the swastika had evened things up after 511 days of front-line combat, by conquering the birthplace of the movement that shamed it.

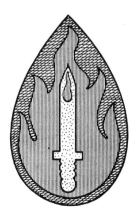

63d Infantry Division

AT THE CASABLANCA CONFERENCE, early in 1943, the Allies vowed to make their enemies "bleed and burn in expiation of their crimes against humanity." That struck the men of the 63d Division, when their outfit was activated the following June, as an estimable idea, and the division promptly adopted the vengeful nickname "Blood and Fire."

After a year and a half of training in the States, the 63d sailed for Europe to do what it could about helping to carry out the Casablanca promise. Late in 1944, the men who wear the blood-tipped dagger thrust into the German lines for the first time.

The first fight of one regiment—the 254th Infantry—was especially notable. Attached to the 3d Infantry Division during the fierce struggle for the Colmar bridgehead on the Seventh Army front from January 22 to February 6, the whole regiment was among units cited for outstanding performance of duty in that sector. Struggling forward through knee-deep snow that concealed deadly land mines, the 254th helped to cut off Colmar from the Rhine in what was officially described as "one of the hardest fought and bloodiest campaigns of the war."

In February, with the whole Division reassembled, the 63d crossed the Saar north of Sarreguemines and led the Seventh Army back onto German soil, from which it had been forced to pull back, and the Division captured the fortress town of Ommersheim. A few weeks later, the 63d led the Army into the lower Siegfried Line on a two-mile front, just south of Saarbrücken.

Early in April, the Blood-and-Fire men destroyed the 17th SS Division, fought through the Hardthauser Woods, crossed the Neckar River, and forced the enemy to retreat to new positions south of the Kocher River.

Then when the Germans in the south began to fall back in disorganization, the 63d was one of the outfits that pursued them relentlessly, striking at the near-beaten enemy forces. It chased the Germans through Württemberg and Bavaria down to the Danube, crossing the river at Günzburg and going on down to Landsberg, at the edge of the Bavarian Alps.

The Germans, who were great ones for burning books, always regarded Heidelberg as their principal seat of learning. It was thus perhaps only justice that the "Blood-and-Fire" Division should have been the American outfit that fought its way into the university city and captured it at the end of March.

Funny thing, too: there wasn't a single book deliberately burned.

65th Infantry Division

THE "BATTLE-AXE" DIVISION was forged in August 1943, and sharpened for nearly two years. Then, on March 7, 1945, it was unsheathed.

Sent into action on the Third Army front in Europe, the 65th relieved the 26th Division along the Saar River, near Saarlautern, in an area that ran from Orscholz to Wadgassen. Crossing the Saar, the Division swung around the flank of Saarbrücken and, late in the month, cleaned up pockets south and west of that city. Then, moving behind speeding armor of the Third Army, the 65th mopped up at Altengottern and at Langensalza, ten miles north of Gotha.

Moving to the east, the Battle-Axe outfit added Hohenfals and Struth to its bag. Near Struth, at the town of Dorna, one 11-man group of 65th soldiers, hopelessly surrounded and terrifically outnumbered, won themselves a place in the Division's history by turning the tables on the Nazis who finally captured them and, before they were through, capturing 150 Germans themselves and killing another 25.

Just before V-E Day, the 65th claimed the distinction of having made the farthest penetration into enemy territory of any Infantry unit on the Western Front—when a patrol of the Intelligence and Reconnaissance Platoon of its 259th Infantry, on May 7, crossed the Ems River at Kronstorf and proceeded on to Unterwinden and Haag, in Austria.

Up to then, the 65th had been extremely active. Moving forward with the Third Army, the Battle-Axers had plunged across the Danube at Kelheim and joined the American forces assaulting the city of Regensburg. When the garrison at Regensburg finally gave up, it surrendered to the 65th. The Division moved on then into the Bavarian Redoubt, and took Passau and Neumarkt. On the afternoon of V-E Day, fittingly, the Battle-Axers met the Russians. Finally, the Division moved to Linz, Austria, under a separate occupation agreement.

66th Infantry Division

"SWINE!"

That being the most popular French designation for German soldiers, it must have pleased the French to see the way the 66th "Black Panther" Infantry Division handled the 50,000 Nazi troops trapped in the St. Nazaire and Lorient pockets.

Given the job of containing these Nazi fighters, the 66th Doughboys penned them in exactly as if they were a herd of swine. The 66th was assigned this important, if not glamorous, mission late in December of 1944, and it stayed on the job until V-E Day. During that time the 50,000 Nazis, all members of crack outfits, made many efforts to break from the trap, but were beaten back by the men and steel of the Black Panthers.

The frustrated Nazis and the Doughs of the 66th had many sharp patrol clashes, and there were frequent artillery duels. But the Nazis stayed put, and few, if any of them managed to escape to fight in the defense of the Reich.

The Nazi troops surrendered to the 66th on May 8, 1945. By this surrender the 66th not only took the arms from the 50,000 Nazis, but liberated 856 square miles of France, and freed 180,-000 civilians who had been held as prisoners by the Germans.

Following V-E Day the Black Panthers were again given a thankless, but very vital job. The Division was assigned to guard three staging areas, including the great port of Marseille. It was

the job of the Black Panthers to see that the ports of embarka-
tion, from which American troops flowed toward home and the
Pacific, were kept running smoothly during the era of redeployment.

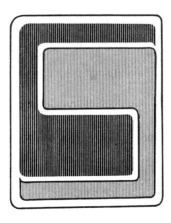

69th Infantry Division

FROM THE MOMENT THE ALLIES landed on the smoking beaches of Normandy on June 6, 1944, everyone knew what one of their principal objectives was—to slash deep into Germany itself and cut the Nazis' defenses in two by joining hands with the Russian armies driving from the eastern front.

More than ten months later, on April 25, 1945, the dream came true.

A patrol of the 69th Division—the "Fighting Sixty-ninth" of this war—jumping from the Division's positions on the Mulde River across the Elbe, climbed to the top of an old tower at Torgau, on the west bank of the Elbe, and saw some Russian soldiers across the river.

A few minutes later American and Russian hands were clasped halfway across a battered bridge that spanned the river, and official contact had been made between the two Allies.

There were other meetings with the Russians by other men of the Fighting Sixty-ninth, but Torgau was dubbed the "official" junction. The Division itself will probably never stop arguing as to which of its units first joined up with the Red Army— but no other division can dispute that honor with the 69th.

The "Fighting Sixty-ninth" first saw action on March 8, in the Siegfried Line, when two regiments crashed the fortified line on a 2,000-yard front. The Doughboys of the 69th took 200 prisoners on their first day in combat, and shortly captured

Rescheid, Jamberg, Dickeerschied, and Honningen, among other towns. That was the official start of the battle for the 69th, but many weeks earlier, while the Division was waiting in France for its chance to show its stuff, four members of the 69th's quartermaster company had made an unofficial start when, on a routine trip to Reims for supplies, they had bagged some Germans hiding out in a French farmhouse.

At the junction of the Moselle and Rhine Rivers, the 69th took the ancient fortress of Ehrenbreitstein, but their first important victory was at Leipzig. There, on April 19, the 69th, along with the 11th Armored Division, finally forced the surrender of fanatical German defenders who fought a last bloody stand at the base of Napoleon's monument until they were blasted out by heavy fire from self-propelled guns.

There are many high points in the 69th's combat chronicle—the capture intact of a 70-ton bridge across the Weser River, and the occupation of dozens of small German towns like Nissmitz and Fürstenwalde and Maidenbressen, for instance—but until something better comes along the Fighting Sixty-ninth, and the Russians who held the other side of the Elbe, will always put Torgau at the top of their list.

April 25 was really a red-letter day.

70th Infantry Division

THE DOUGHBOYS OF THE 70TH ("Trailblazer") Infantry Division wear an axe blade on their shoulder patch, and they were axemen to the Wehrmacht in Europe.

From the time they plunged into the European conflict in December 1944, until the Nazi capitulation, the Trailblazers never took a backward step. One of the Division's memorable moments came less than two months after its men had landed at Marseille. In February, working in concert with other Seventh Army outfits along the Alsace-Lorraine border, the Trailblazers launched a drive that culminated in the capture of Spicheren Heights, known to Nazis as "Hitler's Holy Ground."

It was at this point, a famous spot in the Franco-Prussian War of 1870, that Hitler first set foot in France following his accession to power. On Christmas Day, during the "phony war" of 1939, Der Führer cautiously advanced a few yards into France and spoke a few words to his followers.

Spicheren Heights overlook the town of Styring-Wendel. In liberating this French city, the Trailblazers also freed nearly 1,000 Allied prisoners of war, predominantly Russian, but including Poles, French, Czechs, and Yugoslavs. This was one of the first, if not the first, deliverances of Allied POWs on the Western Front.

Early in March, a resumption of the offensive carried the

70th to the south bank of the Saar River, and two of its Infantry regiments—the 276th and 274th—claim the honor of having first put men across the vital stream. On March 20 the city of Saarbrücken fell to the 275th Infantry. At the same time the remaining Trailblazer units swarmed through the formidable Siegfried Line defenses along the north bank of the Saar to take Volkingen and other important Saarland cities and towns.

Late in March advance elements of the 70th met men of the 26th Infantry Division and effected their junction with the Third Army.

The Trailblazers first saw combat on December 28, 1944, when the three regiments were committed in defensive positions along the west bank of the Rhine in northern Alsace. Once in the line, the Doughs of the 70th took part in some of the bitterest actions of that portion of the German offensive (simultaneous with the Ardennes breakthrough) which saw the Nazis attempt to drive south from the Bitche sector in the hope of cutting off the entire Seventh Army, west of the Saverne Pass.

In this action, it was often a battle by battalions.

At Wingen, a village in the mountains south of Bitche, Trailblazers surrounded and sealed off 1,000 SS troops, and cleaned them out in a hard three-day battle. This broke the point of the northern prong of the German drive. The men who did this job were men who had been on European soil less than a month.

After the reduction of the Saar Basin, troops of the 70th engaged in occupational duties at Otterberg, Bad Kreuznach, Frankfurt, and Oranienstein, near Limburg-on-Lahn.

71st Infantry Division

"TRAVEL WITH US and meet everyone in Europe."

That was the slogan of the 71st Infantry Division when V-E Day came around.

One of the most popular pastimes of the 71st Doughs was trying to figure out just where they had been, and under what commands they had served.

When the 71st reached France in February 1945, it was with the Seventh Army. It then was switched to the Fifteenth Army, and later served with the Third Army. It was with the XV Corps and the XXII Corps. As one GI quipped, "We just missed the K-9 Corps."

In its time in action the 71st served alongside the 100th, 42d, 44th, 3d, 104th, 26th, and 5th Infantry Divisions, and the 10th and 12th Armored outfits.

The 71st went into action in the bitter cold of March 1945, and for 15 days its mission was the destruction of German pockets west of the Rhine. When the 71sters hit the Siegfried Line, they kept right on going, breaching the famed defense wall to capture Pirmasens. When the Doughs swept through this city they liberated 8,000 slave laborers.

The 71st then drove across the Hardt Mountains and the Rhine plains, and cleaned up Nazi resistance on the west bank of the Rhine near Ludwigshafen and Speyer.

One of the most important achievements of the 71st was the

cutting of the Berlin-Munich highway, main escape route from the capital of the Bavarian mountains. It was in this drive that the 71st bagged upwards of 30 German generals.

The Division crossed the Danube in assault boats at several places east of Regensburg. It was in on the capture of Mannheim, aiding the 44th Division. This city fell when, after military officials had refused to heed the mayor's request that the city yield to the Americans, the Yanks turned 26 battalions of artillery fire on the place.

On V-E Day the 71st was south of Linz, Austria, on the Enns River, and later it moved to Augsburg, Germany.

75th Infantry Division

THE GERMANS couldn't have been blamed if they had thought the American Army had at least two 75th Divisions.

The 75th—there was only one—bounded back and forth so much along the European battlefront from January to May 1945, that observing its progress was a good deal like watching a lively tennis match.

Reaching the European Theater in November 1944, nineteen months after its activation, the 75th began fighting on January 1 in the Battle of the Bulge, and stayed in action there for 26 cold and bitter days. Crossing the Salm River, the 75th moved into the north flank of the Ardennes salient in Belgium, cleared Salmchâteau and Bech, and helped take the important bastion of Vielsalm. The Division also was one of the American outfits that fought at St. Vith.

The 75th swept down to the Seventh Army front, in the Colmar–Breisach area. At the end of January, the Division was busily engaged in that part of Alsace, where it eliminated a pocket of resistance between Colmar and the Rhine.

By March 1 the 75th was up north again, in defensive positions on the west bank of the Maas River in Holland. On March 7th—there they go again—the Division jumped from Venlo, Holland, to Bryell, Germany. After much patrol activity east of the Rhine, the 75th crossed the river on March 24, and a week later launched its first big attack on the other side.

From then on, the much-travelled 75th fought in the Hotten–Grandmenil sector, took Witten, and conducted extensive mopping-up operations in the north corner of the Ruhr pocket, at Eckern and other points.

On V-E Day the 75th was at Lütgen, Germany, and shortly thereafter it set up occupation headquarters at Werdohl. Later it moved out to operate an assembly area for other troops being returned to the United States.

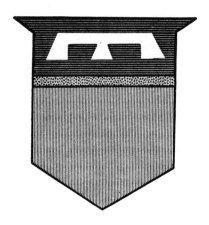

76th Infantry Division

IN THE ARMY, a holiday can't often be celebrated in the orthodox way, but sometimes it's a pretty special day anyhow. For the "Liberty Bell" Division, for instance, Thanksgiving in 1944 will always have great significance. It was on that day that the 76th, after 29 months' training in the U. S., finally pushed off for Europe.

The 76th was the first Allied division to enter Germany via Luxembourg. In February 1945, the men who sometimes, jokingly referring to the design of their shoulder patch, call themselves the "Bell Telephone" outfit, went into action. (Actually, the three-pronged "label" on the 76th's insignia is a replica of a medieval design used to indicate the eldest son of a family.) Near Bitburg, Germany, on the Third Army front, they cleared the east bank of the Prüm River, went south to take Irrel, Wolsfeld, and Alsdorf, and then drove a salient across the highway linking Bitburg with Trier and contributing greatly to Trier's ultimate capture.

Joining up with the 10th Armored Division, the Liberty Bells made two crossings of the Moselle River, pushing to 17 miles northwest of Trier, and adding such towns as Butzweiler, Binsfeld, Herscherforst, and Arrenrath to their bag. Near Kamburg, the 76th reached the Saale River, and went across it to clear the city of Zeitz (population 30,000), 20 miles southwest of Leipzig. Then came a mission of mercy—the rescue of Allied prisoners penned in at the Königstein Fortress. As the winter drew on, the Division found itself mixed up in some heavy fighting. In one sector, 3,000 meters square, the 76th cleaned out a total of 131 enemy pillboxes.

Toward the end of the war the Liberty Bells fought in the Gera area and, just before V-E Day, established a bridgehead across the Mulde River. By that time, the 76th had taken 33,000 prisoners.

When American forces began to pull back out of occupied territory assigned to the Russians, the 76th was the first division to make such a withdrawal, retiring from Chemnitz to the west bank of the Mulde and taking up positions south and west of Zwichau. By July, the Division was on guard duty at Hoff.

77th Infantry Division

GENERAL DOUGLAS MACARTHUR, an old football player himself, gave the job of pulling the Statue of Liberty play on the Japs at Leyte to the outfit best fitted to execute it—the 77th Infantry Division, whose men carry Miss Liberty on their shoulders.

In one of the most daring operations of the Pacific War— General Walter Krueger, Sixth Army commander, admitted that it might have turned into an "American Dunkirk"—the Statue of Liberty Division made a landing behind the main Japanese defense line on Ormoc Bay.

Striking shortly after dawn, three years to the day after Pearl Harbor, the Doughboys of the 77th caught the Japs completely by surprise, and, in the heavy battles which followed, broke the back of the enemy defense of Leyte.

Ground opposition was light in the initial stages of the landing, but heavy Japanese air attacks pounded the Doughboys the first few nights. Three days later Ormoc, hub of the Nip defense, was captured, and the 77th pushed on against heavy opposition to join other elements of the X Corps. This junction ended organized Jap resistance, and on Christmas Day, 1944, the island was declared secure.

With the Guam and Leyte campaigns under its belt, the 77th could have been excused for thinking it had seen Pacific fighting at its roughest. But the worst was yet to come. From Leyte, the 77th plunged into the savage, bloody battle for Okinawa, right in the Jap's front yard. Here the Doughs of the 77th ran into the heaviest artillery fire of the Pacific war. They were plastered day and night by field pieces of all sizes. The enemy's pillboxes were superior to any he had used at Tarawa and Saipan. And facing the Division's front was Shuri, central fortress of the Jap defense line on southern Okinawa. Innumerable ridges, all of which bristled with Nip defenses, blocked the way to the high ground commanding Shuri. The Doughs, working with tanks, flamethrowers, and dynamite charges, finally dislodged the enemy, but not without heavy losses.

The 77th was also given the job of taking Ie Shima, tiny island of the Ryukyu group. It proved to be just as mean as Okinawa. The Japs managed to survive the terrific naval and air bombardment that preceded the landing of the Statue of Libertymen, and when the Doughs hit the beaches charged from their caves and tunnels.

It was on Ie Shima that Ernie Pyle, most beloved of correspondents, was killed. He went ashore with the 77th Division to record the agonies of the foot soldier, and was killed by machine-gun fire.

The 77th began its fight against the Japs in July 1944 when it landed on Orote Peninsula, Guam, and relieved the 4th Marines. Within 8 days, the Division had occupied the eastern beaches, and followed up by capturing Yona, San Antonio, and Barrigada. The Division was in action 21 days and advanced 18 miles against a trapped and desperate enemy.

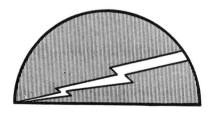

78th Infantry Division

You will never convince a surviving member of the late Wehrmacht that lightning can't strike twice.

He knows it can, because he and his fellow Nazi soldiers were struck again and again by the 78th ("Lightning") Infantry Division.

It was in the morning mist of March 8, 1945, that the 78th, made up chiefly of men from Ohio, Illinois, Pennsylvania, and New York, struck its most brilliant blow. While tracer bullets ripped the air in wild zig-zag patterns, shells splashed against the abutments, and flying metal ricocheted off steel girders, Lightning Doughboys crossed the Ludendorff Bridge at Remagen—and earned the honor of being the first infantry division troops to span the Rhine.

The crossing marked an important turning point in the war against Germany. The "impregnable" Siegfried Line had been torn open; the German defenses along the Roer had been smashed, and the stage was set for the final, crushing blow of the Allied offensive.

It was fitting that the 78th—the Division which, by its capture of Schwammenauel Dam, had made possible the great drive to the Rhine—was the first to cross the Nazis' last great natural obstacle.

The capture of the dam played a tremendous part in enabling the Allies to move onto the offensive after Rundstedt's mighty counteroffensive had failed. Its 22,000,000,000 gallons of water, once unleashed by the German demolitions, would be sufficient not only to submerge and destroy all the towns along the Roer from Heimbach to Doermund, but to sweep away like matchsticks men and equipment in a river-crossing operation. Its capture was imperative.

The 78th took the dam, but only after one of the fiercest battles of the war. The attack was launched in mid-winter, with the men ploughing through waist-deep snowdrifts. Fortified positions and pillboxes studded the path to the dam. The Infantrymen worked 100 yards behind the artillery as it smacked at some of the heaviest fortifications in Germany. The 78th Doughs worked from town to town, and the fight in each one was the same. They moved from hedgerow to hedgerow, from cellar to cellar, from rubble heap to rubble heap. The final city assaulted was the much-attacked, never captured stronghold of Schmidt. The Lightnings thrust aside their weariness. The prize was only a few miles beyond Schmidt. The Lightnings fought their way through savage fire to the dam. While the fight raged unabated, engineers explored the dam for demolitions, knowing that 22,000,000,000 gallons of water were straining against the structure and that even as they searched a fuse might be burning toward a charge. The dam was taken intact.

Following seizure of the dam, the Division received a commendation from Major General C. R. Huebner, V Corps commander, which stressed the strategic importance of the accomplishment "without which further contemplated winter operations against the enemy on the northern front would have been impossible."

The Lightnings, who did not go overseas until October 1944, got their first crack at the Germans in early December, when they went in the line nine miles southeast of Aachen. Their first take-off was against the Siegfried Line. Their mission was to take the towns of Bickerath, Rollesbroich, Simmerath, Witzfall, and Kesternich—all lying within the belt of fortifications. By nightfall all but Kesternich had fallen. Three days of furious fighting ensued before this key town capitulated. It was near Kesternich that 70 men of the 310th Regiment were trapped in a cellar. They refused to surrender. Nearly every man in the Division—including cooks and clerks—volunteered to go to their rescue, and one group of cooks made several valiant attempts and almost turned the trick. Finally, a patrol reached the trapped men and got them out.

The 78th was in action only a short time, but the men who wear the lightning on their shoulder proved to the world that they were worthy successors to the men of the 78th in World War I, who performed so brilliantly in the St. Mihiel drive and the great Meuse-Argonne offensive.

79th Infantry Division

THE SYMBOL OF THE FIGHTING FRENCH was the Cross of Lorraine.

And in the summer of 1944 many a Frenchman was freed from the bondage of Naziism by the Americans who wear that cross—the 79th Infantry Division.

There were cheers, and flowers, and wine for all the liberating GIs of all our Divisions in Europe, but no outfit was ever more warmly greeted by a whole country than was the 79th by the grateful citizens of Cherbourg, La Haye-du-Puits, Lessay, Le Mans, Avranches, Reims, Charmes, Lunéville, and a dozen other cities on the division's long path of liberation.

The Cross of Lorraine was first carried ashore at Utah Beach on American shoulders on D-plus-6. Four months later, a German division, in an order to its subordinate units, warned them to watch out for the 79th—"one of the best attack divisions in the U. S. Army."

That had been true in World War I, when the 79th stormed Montfaucon and, in 30 hours of hellish fighting, had started the Kaiser's armies on their way to defeat.

And it became equally evident in World War II as soon as the 79th was given its first important mission: a major share in the assault on Cherbourg. While its 314th Infantry Regiment scaled the tough sides of Fort du Roule, on the outskirts of the port, patrols of the 313th sneaked into the city and later the rest of the regiment followed up, smashing through Cherbourg street by street and house by house, and winning for the Division the proud right to claim—First in Cherbourg.

Cherbourg surrendered on July 26 and the next day the 79th, having tasted only briefly the fruits of liberation, was on its way to La Haye-du-Puits, nerve center of the German supply system for the enemy forces in northern France. Through hedgerows honeycombed with artillery and automatic weapons, and despite dug-in enemy tanks raking them at pointblank range, the Cross of Lorraine men swarmed into the town and took it on July 8. They headed south through Avranches and Fougères, and southeast to Le Mans, where, after bridging the Sarthe River, they helped to close the Falaise pocket.

Swinging east, the 79th raced ahead of all other forces toward the Seine, reaching it at the ruined city of Mantes-Gassicourt. No other American outfit reached the Seine as soon, and the 79th, by getting there and holding the rubble of Mantes-Gassicourt, greatly facilitated the liberation of Paris. The Germans were stunned by this swift dash of the Cross of Lorraine; they thought at first that the 79th had suddenly become airborne and had been dropped near the Seine. Recovering from their surprise they hit the Division with Nebelwerfers and a revived Luftwaffe, but it didn't get them anywhere.

Shifted to the First Army front in Belgium, the 79th set off in high gear and in 72 hours had crossed the Somme and was ready to fight in Belgium, 180 miles away, after making what a corps commander called "one of the fastest opposed advances of comparable distance by an infantry division in warfare." Later the Cross of Lorraine was shifted far to the south, on the Seventh Army flank, and fought at the Meurthe River, in the Forêt de Parroy, in the city of Lunéville, and across the Rhine deep into Germany.

After the 79th had driven the Germans out of their positions in the Saverne Gap and Sarrebourg, late in 1944, General Patch told the division, "You have achieved a significant victory. I have full confidence in your ability to continue your relentless pursuit until the final victory."

That was just what the 79th did.

80th Infantry Division

"You can't say too much for them."

That was the tribute "brass" paid to the 80th Infantry Division Doughboys after they had broken through a ring of German lead and steel to help rescue the 101st Airborne Division, never-say-die defenders of Bastogne.

Christmas Day, side by side with tanks of the 4th Armored, Infantrymen of the "Blue Ridge" Division began to batter forward toward the besieged 101st. Through murderous opposition, over frozen, snow-crusted terrain, they bent their heads to bullet and blizzard, and advanced 9 miles. Next day the gap between rescuers and trapped was reduced to 4,000 yards. A Blue Ridge patrol, working at night, slipped through the Nazi lines to meet up with an outpost of the 101st, and gather information concerning German strength and displacement.

With this information, the Doughs of the 80th and the 4th tankers, drove forward, scorning withering artillery, Nebelwerfer, and small-arms fire. They chased the Germans from ridge to ridge, from pillbox to pillbox and, on December 28, knifed through to the lines of the 101st. Relief of Bastogne was completed, Rundstedt's hope for a major breakthrough was finished, and the men of the 80th could proudly reassert their motto: "Ever Forward."

It was no untried division that achieved the drive to Bastogne. The 80th had been in action since it landed on Utah

Beach, in France, early in August. A few days after it hit France, the 80th began fighting at Le Mans, and aided in stemming the powerful armored counterattack by five panzer divisions which sought to cut the Third Army's supply line at Avranches.

Under new orders, the Blue Ridgers were thrown into the battle of the Argentan-Falaise Gap.

They were told to take Argentan and the high ground north of the city. This strongpoint was held by a panzer division, a Luftwaffe battalion, and Storm Troopers supported by artillery and numerous self-propelled guns. Just before midnight of August 19, the city was blasted by artillery. The Blue Ridgers stormed into the burning objective. Surging north from this point, the Doughs of the Blue Ridge had a field day mopping up the wreckage of the once proud German Seventh Army.

After this hard blow to the Wehrmacht, the Division once again became a part of the Third Army, swung south of Paris and spearheaded the Allied drive across France.

The Blue Ridgers crossed the Meuse and, with history repeating itself, rolled into St.Mihiel where, 26 years ago, during the same month, the World War I 80th had fought. Ahead was the heavily fortified Moselle River. Loading on a small stream that runs into the Moselle, the 80th crossed without a shot being fired, and the Third Army's spearhead was ready to run wild. In the later stages of this battle the 80th's artillery commander, Brigadier General Edmund W. Searby, was killed while fighting in the front line with the Doughboys.

In November of 1944, the 80th attacked the Maginot Line. Before its men were relieved by the 6th Armored Division forward elements of the 80th had penetrated the German frontier less than five miles from Saarbrücken.

After 102 days of contact with the enemy, the Blue Ridgers were withdrawn on December 7 for a rest.

Then came Bastogne.

True to their motto, the men of the 80th moved "Ever Forward."

81st Infantry Division

WILDCAT CREEK, a tiny stream that flows through Fort Jackson, South Carolina, inspired the first shoulder patch to be worn by any division in the United States Army.

The 81st Infantry Division took its nickname from the creek, and, when it sailed for France in 1918, its men wore a cloth patch on their left shoulders featuring a silhouette of a wildcat on an olive drab circle.

The patch caused much comment by men of other divisions, and they questioned the right of the Doughboys of the 81st thus to distinguish themselves. The matter was finally brought to the attention of General John J. Pershing, and "Black Jack," after an investigation, ruled that the Wildcat Division could keep its patch, and suggested that all other units adopt distinctive insignia.

The Wildcats fought with honor against the Germans, and a generation later the fighting men of the new 81st Division were clawing at the Japanese in the Pacific.

The World War II Wildcats began their drive against the Japanese in September of 1944. After training in Oahu and the Solomon Islands, the Wildcats sailed for their first combat mission—the capture of Angaur Island in the Palaus. They stormed ashore on September 17, and the conquest of Angaur was speedily accomplished as troops drove through Japanese defenses to the western shore, cutting the island in two and driving the enemy into isolated pockets of resistance. Angaur was declared secure on September 20, and mopping-up operations began on the remnants of the Japanese garrison which had fortified itself for a death stand on the high ground in the northwest corner of the island.

After 35 consecutive days of steady fighting, the last Japanese cave was entered, and every Jap on the island was a dead Jap.

Elements of the 81st Division were with the 1st Marine Division in the assault on Peleliu Island, and fought alongside the Leathernecks in the bloody and costly battle for this rocky Pacific pile. On Peleliu, the Japs literally had to be rooted from their deep caves on the precipitous slopes of the jagged cliffs. The Wildcats scaled the slopes to get at the Nips with bayonets, grenades, and dynamite charges, all the while undergoing merciless machine-gun and mortar fire.

The Wildcats mopped up Ngesebus, Kongaru, and Garakayo Islands. They made the first landing on Ulithi, later the Navy's huge Pacific fleet base.

In all these operations the Wildcats killed 5,676 Japanese and took 344 Japs and Koreans prisoner.

In the summer of 1945, the 81st moved to the central Philippines. And later on up into Japan, the end of a long road.

82nd Airborne Division

During the last war, a sergeant named Alvin York—while his Division and the 28th were going to the rescue of the Lost Battalion of the 77th—captured 132 Germans and made himself and his outfit, the 82nd Infantry Division, known to all Americans. The "All-American" Division began this war as an Infantry Division, too, under the leadership of General Omar Bradley, but on August 15, 1942, it was redesignated the 82nd Airborne Division and began training for the special role it was to play in Allied operations in Sicily, Italy, France, Holland, Belgium, and Germany.

The 82nd left the United States in April 1943, and sailed for Casablanca, where it trained while the Tunisian campaign was drawing to a close. The Sicilian campaign was the first one in which an entire airborne division—the 82nd—was scheduled to take part. The mission started tragically, and momentarily jeopardized the future of all airborne operations, when several of the planes, slightly off course and the victims of faulty recognition signals, were fired upon by friendly antiaircraft gunners, with substantial casualties in planes and men.

On June 9, 1943, the 505th Regimental Combat Team, reinforced, tumbled out over Sicily at midnight. The rest of the All-Americans were held in reserve. It was a tough job, but doubly so that night. Tricky winds played hob with aerial navigation. Parachutists scattered along a 50-mile stretch. After landing, and for the next few days, the airborne troops fought a slashing guerrilla action, ferreting out and destroying German and Italian forces. Scattered throughout the lines of the British Army, some All-Americans helped take Comiso, Noto, and Ragusa. Fighting as they went, the men of the 82nd reassembled by foot, mule, bicycle, and truck.

In September of 1943 elements of the 82nd blossomed out over Salerno behind the enemy lines and, by effective operations in the rear, seriously disrupted the movement of enemy supplies to the beachhead area. Later the All-American units swung over to protect the east flank of the Fifth Army, and when the rest of that Army marched into Naples, three weeks after the landings, the 82nd proudly led the way.

Shifted back to England for rigorous pre-invasion training, the 82nd's next combat mission was its most important of all. Stars blinked overhead on the morning of June 6, 1944, when, hours before the Normandy invasion proper began, parachutists of the 82nd fell into hedgerows from Cherbourg to the deep mainland. In two days the Division had captured three towns and crossed the Merderet River. In six more days the 82nd had taken Ham, thus ensuring the security of the beachhead, and had set the stage for the capture of the Cherbourg peninsula. Although airborne operations are normally short, the Division official history reads: ". . . 35 days of action without relief, without replacements . . . every mission accomplished . . . no ground gained ever relinquished . . ." One company came out of the line with 16 men, and most of the Division units were cited for their work.

Two months later, under 38-year-old Major General James M. Gavin, parachute and glider Infantrymen of the 82nd struck again, in the Nijmegen section of Holland, preventing the Germans from breaking through at the Maas River, and endangering Allied operations in that area. Following the Division's work in Holland, Lieutenant General Sir Miles C. Dempsey, British Second Army commander, paid this tribute to General Gavin and his men: "I'm proud to be commanding general of the greatest Division in the world today."

Von Rundstedt launched his great counteroffensive. To Division headquarters came a request from SHAEF: Could the

Division move out in 24 hours and get close to Bastogne? Twenty-three hours later the 82nd was in position 150 miles away, moved by truck. A prime German objective was Liège. The All-Americans were asked to hold an area southwest of the town. They held it a week against overwhelming odds. Another mission was to help provide a withdrawal route for the 28th and 106th divisions which had been cut off. They provided the escape route. In January of 1945 the 82nd hit the Siegfried Line and cracked it three days later. As the war ended, it was fighting with the British Second Army at Wittenburg, and subsequently it followed the 2d Armored Division into Berlin.

83d Infantry Division

THERE WAS A COLONEL at the fortress of St.Malo—the one they called the "Mad Colonel"—who didn't want to surrender, and to the east there were 20,000 armed German soldiers of every rank who didn't want to surrender, either. That is, they didn't want to until the 83d Division came along. Then they had to. Colonel Von Aulock was the defiant commander who, in the fall of 1944, decided to hold out, and it looked as if he might for an indefinite time until the "Thunderbolt" Division laid siege to his stronghold and caused him to think better of his initial decision. A few weeks later, when the Division captured 20,000 Germans at one swoop in France, while covering the right flank of the Third Army in the Loire River Valley, the Thunderbolts set a record for the number of prisoners taken by the Allies up to that time on the European continent.

The 83d hoped to get into the battle of Normandy right at the start, but rough weather kept it out in the English Channel for a week, and it finally hit the beaches on D-plus-12. Plunging into the hedgerows, it moved inland to the swamps of Carentan, to relieve the 101st Airborne Division which had jumped just before H-hour on D-day. On the Fourth of July, the 83d launched its first big offensive. With the 9th and 90th Infantry Divisions, it broke through to the St.Lô–Coutances highway, moved early in August by truck to Avranches, and then headed west to take care of the stubborn residents of St. Malo, which fell on August 17.

Operating in the Loire Valley from August 22 to September 20, the 83d covered a 200-mile line from St. Nazaire to Auxerre, made a junction with the Seventh Army, and delivered its celebrated haul of 20,000 Supermen to the Allies. Late in September the division, as part of the Third Army, swung northeastward for the drive through France and Luxembourg. In Luxembourg, relieving the 5th Armored and 28th Infantry Divisions, the 83d made a lasting impression on the civilians with its lively dance band. It didn't have much time, however, for rest or frivolity. Early in December it was moved into the Hürtgen Forest to relieve the 4th Infantry Division, and from there it fought its way to the western bank of the Roer, near Düren. And then came the Ardennes counteroffensive.

Ordered to Rochefort, the 83d found itself fighting in waist-high snow. Morphine syrettes froze, automatic weapons wouldn't function, and the soldiers of the Division suffered from the bitter cold. They stuck to their guns—sometimes literally—and helped turn back the enemy assault. A month later they were assigned to the Ninth Army and, on March 1, approached the Rhine and took Neuss, just outside of Düsseldorf. They were credited with being the first American division to reach the lower Rhine, and, after patrols had made several crossings of the river to probe the enemy defenses on the other side, the whole Division swept across on March 30. Given the job of cleaning up pockets by-passed by the 2d Armored, the Thunderbolts accomplished that mission and then did some by-passing of their own, slicing through the Ruhr Valley and driving for the transportation center of Hamm.

Marching virtually unopposed into the blasted Hamm rail-yards, the 83d seized so many abandoned vehicles that it was able completely to motorize itself, and it raced east to the province of Brunswick, moving so fast with its borrowed transportation that at one point it outstripped the speedy 2d Armored. Swinging southeast, the 83d pushed 215 miles from the Rhine to the Elbe, which it reached at Barby, just south of the 2nd Armored's bridgehead. On its way, the 83d in 14 days captured 24,000 Germans and liberated 75,000 Allied prisoners.

Most of the men of the 83d, when it fought in Italy and France in 1918 had originally come from Ohio, and the Division's shoulder patch is a monogram of the letters of that state. In this war the Division's personnel has been drawn from all over, but the men still like the old patch, and they like to spell out the words for which the letters now stand—"One Hot Infantry Outfit."

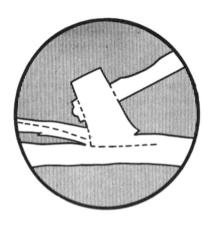

84th Infantry Division

WHEN IT FOUGHT IN FRANCE during the last war, the 84th called itself the "Lincoln" Division. When this war started, the men of the outfit were calling themselves the "Railsplitters." But not long after they bumped into the German Army on the Siegfried Line, the Nazis had a new name for them—and it had nothing to do with the biographical background of Abraham Lincoln.

The Germans called them the Hatchet Men.

It was November 18, 1944, when the 84th first struck. Only a few weeks before it had been in the United States. After sailing to England and training at Winchester—where a few men were detached to go to the Continent and help speed supplies over the famous Red Ball Highway—Railsplitters embarked for France and were rushed to the Siegfried Line. Then began two months of savage fighting during which the 84th took 112 German pillboxes and bunkers in the Siegfried Line, and helped to crush Rundstedt's counteroffensive in the Ardennes. It was as notable a start as any fighting outfit could hope to have.

Assigned to the British Second Army, the 84th set its sights upon Geilenkirchen, a mining and transportation center with a population of 20,000. The 334th Infantry jumped off first, with Prummern as its objective. The regiment was supposed to have armored support, but its tanks bogged down in the mud. That didn't stop the Doughboys; they went in anyhow. Then the 333d Infantry joined in the fray, and Geilenkirchen fell on the 19th shortly followed by Suggerath, Lindern, Beeck, and—in one of the war's best examples of infantry-artillery teamwork—Leiffarth. As the 84th pushed toward this city, the Infantry moved forward confidently a scant 50 yards behind the crashing shells of its own big guns. Mullendorf was the scene of the Railsplitters' last operations in the Siegfried Line sector, and the campaign was fittingly concluded when a battalion commander strode out of Nazi headquarters puffing a big cigar, with a captured swastika slung over his shoulder.

On January 2, while the German counteroffensive in the Ardennes was at its height, the 84th was rushed back to help and made a gallant stand south of Marche. With no flank support, the Railsplitters held their ground and beat off one fierce enemy thrust after another. Shifted later to the north side of the German bulge, under the First Army, the Division set off a counterattack with the 2nd Armored Division. Snow temporarily stopped most of the "Hell on Wheels" tanks, but it couldn't stop the Infantry. One bunch of Doughboys—the 1st Battalion of the 335th Infantry—made an urgent request for hundreds of suits of long winter underwear. Donning these over their combat uniforms, they sneaked across the white fields and took the enemy completely by surprise. By January 16 the 84th had rolled into Houffalize, and on that day, near Ourthe, one of its units joined up with the 11th Armored Division—thus officially linking the First and Third Armies and closing the gap that had separated them in the Ardennes salient.

Moved secretly to an assembly area in Holland, the Railsplitters swept across the Roer River on February 23, and then, led by a motorized task force built around the 334th Infantry, they roared forward—overrunning a German officers' replacement pool, not even bothering to stop to take many prisoners, capturing one city's whole police force intact, taking Dulken, Krefeld, and Moers, and ending up at the Rhine. They almost got to the other side via a tunnel connected to a mine shaft at Homburg, but the tunnel had been mined. After crossing on the surface, they went on over the Weser River, took Erbeck, captured a Nazi arms factory built 350 feet into the side of a cliff, and drove into Hannover. Farther on, at Brunswick, they consolidated forces with the 5th Armored Division, and the two outfits joined the British to wipe out an enemy pocket along the Elbe south of Hamburg.

After V-E Day, with headquarters at Hannover, the Railsplitters spent weeks trying to help displaced persons get started on their way home.

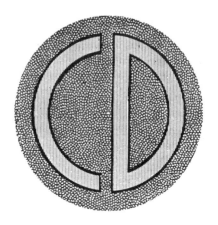

85th Infantry Division

On April 10, 1944, the Germans who had the job of manning defensive positions in the Italian mountains found a new American outfit deployed against them—the 85th Division. It had been called the "Custer" Division ever since 1917, when its soldiers trained at Camp Custer, Michigan. By the time the 85th had bowled over the enemy defenders of the Gustav Line, of Rome, of the Arno River, of the Gothic Line, of the Po River, and of the Brenner Pass, far to the north, the Germans had a new name for the outfit.

They called it the "Elite Assault" Division.

In this war, there wasn't any Custer's Last Stand. Time after time the 85th found itself fighting against seemingly hopeless odds—and there were a few units that had bad luck, like the platoon that was found wiped out, with German bodies piled up all around it, during the breaching of the Gustav Line—but the Division kept on moving slowly forward during the long, grim, and sometimes heartbreaking Italian campaign. When it added up its prisoners after the Germans surrendered on May 2, 1945, the total came to 27,429.

The 85th began to arrive in Italy in the middle of March 1944, and by the end of the month the Division was assembled as a unit. Two weeks later it took over the Allied sector near Minturno and found itself playing a prominent part in the Allied offensive to break through the Gustav Line, made contact with our forces hemmed in at Anzio, and raced to Rome. The attack began on May 11, and after four days of bitter initiation to war, the 85th had beaten off numerous counterattacks and had cracked the line. Speeding north, the Division trampled over the famed Hermann Goering Panzer Division, and triumphantly entered Rome on June 4. The 85th went right on out the other side of the city and pursued the Germans for 40 miles before being relieved.

The Custermen had it relatively quiet during the summer, but in mid-September they were given the job of hacking away at the German positions in the Gothic Line. The towering mountains at Altuzzo, Verruca, and Pratone were in their sector, and on September 17 Altuzzo, the keystone of the line, had fallen to the 85th. Speeding on to the north, the Division chased the Germans for 45 days of running fighting, through the Santerno River Valley, across many mountains, and onto the slopes of Monte Mezzano, at the threshold of the Po Valley.

Early in 1945, the 85th held the Monte Grande sector of the winter defense line, with a crack German parachute division facing it. The stalemate was broken on April 18 when the Custer men swept through Gesso, Tignano, and Casalecchio, advanced into the Po plain, and dashed pell mell through disorganized enemy formations. The 85th flung itself across the Po River, though no bridges were available in its sector, on rafts, DUKWs, and anything else that would float. It moved quickly through Verona, crossed the now unoccupied Adige Line—last German defensive position in Italy—slashed into the Alps, and, by sealing off the Brenner Pass, trapped the remnants of the German Tenth Army, who surrendered en masse.

Even after the Germans gave up, the 85th wasn't through. Its men uncovered millions of dollars' worth of gold and valuable works of art, and released from imprisonment a group of international celebrities the Germans had hidden at Lago di Braies, in the Alps, including Martin Niemöller, Leon Blum, Kurt Schuschnigg, and Fritz Thyssen.

86th Infantry Division

LAST IN AND FIRST OUT—that was the unique record of the "Black Hawk" Division on the Western Front. But the men of the 86th didn't expect to be finished with war when, a few weeks after V-E Day, they were rushed from Austria to the French coast and then to New York, where they were acclaimed on June 17 as the first division to return from the war.

There had been a good reason for their speedy homecoming. They were on their way to Japan. They got there with less trouble than they had originally expected; their Pacific job turned out to be not battle, but occupation.

The Black Hawks fought for only 42 days in Europe. But during that brief spell of action they earned respect from friend and foe alike for their speed, maneuverability, and courage. The 86th served under four armies—the Fifteenth, First, Seventh and Third—claimed to be the first of all our divisions to cross the Danube River, and fought with distinction in mopping-up operations in the Ruhr pocket.

Activated in December 1942, the Black Hawks trained in the United States for more than two years, and finally embarked for Europe in February 1945. Landing at Le Havre, the 86th moved across France and Germany by train and truck, finally arriving at Cologne near the end of March. There a few units of the Division saw their first action, relieving elements of the

8th Infantry Division in position along the west bank of the Rhine.

Then the Black Hawks moved south along the river, crossing it at Bonn, travelling deep into Germany, and taking such towns as Ober Veizhelde, Attendorn, and Hohenlimberg, Gosseldorf, Weizemburg and Echstatt. At Echstatt, the Black Hawks liberated a large number of Allied prisoners of war.

By April 26 the Division had moved to a position just outside of Ingolstadt, close to the Danube. Under persistent enemy artillery fire, the Black Hawks drove through the city and onto the banks of the Danube, spearheading the advance of the Third Army on the river. That evening, while American tanks lined the river banks and poured shells into the enemy lines across the water, and Black Hawk mortars and machine guns threw thousands of rounds of steel into the dusk, Doughboys of the 86th shoved off from the east side of the Danube and secured a bridgehead on the opposite bank.

The Black Hawks kept pushing forward across the river until they had established positions, and then they had to fight off an enemy counterattack designed to throw them back into the water. They held their ground.

Fighting against Germans who knew the jig was almost up but still were determined not to give in without a struggle, and against Hungarian Storm Troopers whom the Nazis had thrown into the battle, the 86th moved forward through Eitensheim, Haag, Altdorf, and Nauhen, in Austria.

At the end of the war in Europe they were in Perwang, after covering ground so rapidly that they left their own kitchens far behind. But they were used to that sort of thing. One Black Hawk unit had had its chow wagon ambushed in the Ruhr pocket. Later, at Ludensheim, they caught up with the Germans who had stolen their rations, and found that the enemy still had a lot of their stuff with them. The Black Hawks got their revenge; they made the Germans eat every bit of the captured hoard—everything except the tin boxes it was packed in.

87th Infantry Division

THE ACORN IS A TRADITIONAL symbol of strength, and before the wearers of the Golden Acorn were through in Europe they had convinced the Germans that the symbolism was more than justified. The Division with the slogan "Stalwart and Strong" had shown itself to be both.

Sailing from the United States on November 1, 1944, the 87th arrived only three weeks later near Metz, on the Third Army front, where General Patton planned to give it its baptism of fire. But Marshal Von Rundstedt changed those plans with his counteroffensive. When Patton rushed over to help the First Army repel the onslaught, the 87th was one of the divisions he took with him to smash the drive. They moved close to where the battered remnants of the 106th Division were reassembling. "When we saw what had been done to them," one 87th man said, "our outfit got together and started working as a team."

By February the 87th was a veteran outfit, used to the tricks of the Germans and accustomed to the bitter climatic conditions on the winter front. Then the Golden Acorns were picked as the spearhead for a Third Army drive toward Luxembourg across the Our River. Under heavy fire from the enemy, the Doughboys crossed the river and drove forward.

During the remainder of February and March, the Division

consolidated its earlier gains and continued to strike lethal blows at the enemy. Early in April the 87th launched a new major thrust.

Moving with lightning speed, the Golden Acorns leaped the Moselle River and charged down on Coblenz. Before the Germans knew what had happened, the city had fallen to the 87th, and the Third Army's drive into the heart of the Rhineland had started. Reaching the Rhine, the 87th once more was in the forefront of battle, and once more it was assigned the job of pushing its way across a river.

This time it wasn't so easy. As the first wave of troops began to sneak across on small boats, the Germans on the opposite shore threw up flares. By their weird light, the enemy hurled in heavy and accurate concentrations of mortar fire on the advancing Americans. Casualties were heavy, but the 87th wouldn't stop. By grit and courage the Golden Acorn soldiers forced their way over the Rhine and pressed forward on the opposite bank.

The Division took many German cities, and the last of the lot was the internationally known sporting resort of Oberhof, in the Black Forest, which the 1st Battalion of the 347th Infantry seized just before the war in Europe ended. "We arrived too late for the skiing and skating," one Golden Acorn Doughboy reported mournfully a few days later, "but the shooting sure as hell was fine."

88th Infantry Division

IN WORLD WAR II towns have been liberated by men in tanks, by paratroopers dropping from the sky, by scout car patrols, and by jeep, but it remained for the Doughboys of the 88th Infantry Division to do the job by bicycle.

Shortly before the cessation of hostilities in Italy, the 2nd Battalion of the 350th Infantry requisitioned bikes from the friendly Italians and, in a "mad" dash from Nogara to San Martino, drove the Nazi troops from the last named city and liberated its citizens.

The 88th, whose Doughs wear a blue cloverleaf formed by two interlocking 8s on their shoulders, was the first all-Selective-Service infantry division committed to combat on any front in this war. The Cloverleaf boys got their first taste of action—and it was a minor one compared to the battles that were to come—when the Division took up positions along the Garigliano River in Italy in March 1944.

This was purely a defensive action, but a week later the Division was given the go-ahead signal and launched its assault on the Gustav Line. Two days later, despite the most savage opposition, the vaunted line was breached, and the Cloverleafs were on the road to Rome, close behind the fleeing Nazis.

The 88th marched into the Eternal City 24 hours after it had become the first liberated capital of World War II. A few weeks rest in Rome and the 88th was on the move again, taking over the missions of the 1st Armored Division, which it had relieved.

This time its goal was the celebrated Gothic Line, and the 88th drove toward it with a relentlessness that brooked no opposition.

Now, began the Division's most savage battle. It entered the Gothic Line action in September, and during the ensuing months suffered its heaviest casualties. It battled unfavorable terrain, miserable weather, and a fanatical enemy. But it kept punching, punching, to capture Mt. La Fine, Belvedere, Gesso, Mt. Acuto, Mt. Capello, Castel del Rio, Mt. Battaglia, and Mt. Grande. Mt. Grande was the nearest point to the Po Valley reached by any Fifth Army outfit until the spring of the following year. During this drive the 88th was exposed to one of the most intense artillery poundings of the entire Italian campaign.

The 88th was ordered to hold up after the Mt. Grande drive, and spent the winter in alternate rest periods and tours in the line. Observing its first combat anniversary on March 5, 1945, the Division had chalked up an offensive advance of 325 miles, captured more than 5,500 prisoners, and destroyed six German divisions and badly mauled half a dozen others.

In April 1945, the 88th went to work again, this time in the North Apennines Po Valley. It took Monterumici, and by the end of the month one of its units had entered Verona, key communication center of the Valley. Not many weeks later it swept into Vicenza, and then on to Nogara, from which it made its bicycle assault on San Martino.

When the war ended in Italy, units of the Division were ordered to make contact with the Seventh Army. This was accomplished a few miles south of the Brenner Pass in May 1945.

During the Po Valley drive the 88th bagged more than 30,000 prisoners in 16 action-packed days.

89th Infantry Division

THE SHOULDER PATCH OF THE 89TH ("Rolling W") Infantry Division is no novelty to the German people. They became acquainted with it in World War I when the Middle West Division (invert the "W" and it becomes an "M"—see?) occupied a section of their country very near the area now being patrolled by the Doughboys wearing the same insignia.

The 89th didn't see as much action against the Nazis as the Rolling Ws did against the Kaiser's forces, but during the brief time its men were in the line they upheld the outfit's slogan "Get It Done." Once committed, they really rolled, and by the time of Nazi capitulation had advanced a total of 350 miles. In this drive the 89th overran scores of Nazi cities, captured more than 20,000 prisoners, and held its own casualty figures to less than 900.

The Division left the United States in January 1945, but did not enter combat until March 12. It was sent into the line near the Sauer River, east of Echternach, and its first shots were fired on enemy soil. No battle-hardened troops ever moved any faster, or attacked more relentlessly, than did the line companies of the 89th. In their first three weeks under fire, the Rolling W Doughboys advanced some 50 miles to the west bank of the Moselle River. On the morning of March 16 the Doughs, in assault boats, stormed across the river to establish a bridgehead through which the 11th Armored Division passed to begin its battle toward the Rhine.

After clearing an area between the Moselle and Glan Rivers, the 89th moved to a new sector for a crossing of the Rhine between the towns of Kestert and Kaub. By noon of March 26, the Rolling Ws had established three bridgeheads, and within a week had completed mopping up in the rough wooded area of the "Bingen Bulge."

Early in April, the 89th moved northeast to start a drive into Thuringia.

Eisenach was the first city to fall, after a bitter defense by SS troops. In the next two weeks the Division moved rapidly across central Germany to the Zwick-Mulde River. The 89th liberated many Allied prisoners in this advance. At Blankenburg 330 Polish women officers were freed. The capture of Zwichau late in April ended the advance, and the Division passed to control of the First Army.

On V-E Day, the Rolling Ws were pushing into Czechoslovakia.

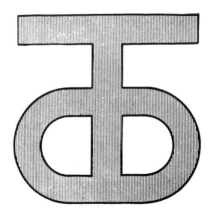

90th Infantry Division

BEFORE D-DAY IN NORMANDY, the initials T-O on the 90th Division's shoulder patch stood for Texas and Oklahoma, home states of most of the outfit's personnel in World War I. Not long after D-day, to the men who wore them, the initials stood for "Tough 'Ombres."

The 90th didn't land without difficulty. One of its troopships was sunk in the English Channel, and a battalion of Infantrymen, with a company of engineers, swam and waded ashore without weapons to enter the fight for the beachhead.

After the landings the Tough 'Ombres, previously untried in battle, fought for 53 straight days. Their first major task was to deepen the wedge driven into France by the aerial assault of the 82nd Airborne Division. The 90th saw heavy fighting at Pont-l'Abbé, Gourbesville, and Portbail. Then, early in July, the Tough 'Ombres went into the misty hell of Forêt de Mont Castre.

For three years the Germans had been using Mont Castre as a maneuver area, and knew the terrain there intimately. Furthermore, it was a heavily fortified sector—the strong point in a line of outposts before the defense line running eastward from Coutances. Facing the Tough 'Ombres were picked German paratroopers and SS men. The 90th struck at Mont Castre on July 3, and battled there for eight days. Camouflaged enemy paratroopers took advantage of the low visibility in the area to raise havoc with the Americans, and one unit of the 90th suffered so heavily that it was compelled to organize a company "J" from an old lot of cooks, clerks, and mechanics.

But the 90th took Mont Castre, and then set off on a new mission. Crossing the Selume River and seizing St. Hilaire-du-Harcouet, the Division began to close the Falaise pocket, and by August 22 the 90th had trapped 12,000 Germans in that sector. During that month, too, the 90th Division took Chambois.

As summer turned into fall, the Division headed east toward Metz, taking part in the attack on that fortified city. By early 1945, the 90th had driven into the Saar, by March it was racing down the east bank of the Rhine, had stormed the gates of Mainz, and had captured the walled city of Boppard.

The war was nearly over, but the 90th wasn't through yet. April saw it fighting south of Eisenach and, after having by-passed armored units, in Barchfeld. It helped take Plauen, and cut Germany virtually in half late in the month by slashing through the rail center of Hof. Just before the final bell rang, the Tough 'Ombres crossed the Czechoslovakian border.

91st Infantry Division

"POWDER RIVER! Let 'er Buck!"

The Powder River is just one of many small streams in Montana, but a lot of Italians and Germans know it well from the war whoop of the 91st Division, first Division to reach the Arno River in Italy, and the outfit that smashed the Gothic Line, took Leghorn, and ended up its wartime travels by making a junction with Marshal Tito's Yugoslav forces in Trieste.

The men who wear the Evergreen on their shoulders—symbol of the Far West whence the 91st's personnel came in World War I, and where the Division trained for both wars— inherited their battle cry from a bunch of Montanans who used it in 1918 to answer a sergeant who wanted to know where they hailed from.

The Powder River began to course up through Italy after the Division had several weeks of realistic training in French Morocco. On June 3, 1944, just one day before the capture of Rome, the Evergreen was first carried into action by the 361st Regimental Combat Team, a few miles south of the Italian capital. The whole Division first swung into battle on July 12, near Chianni, as the Fifth Army began its march on the Arno River. Germans entrenched in prepared positions looked down from the mountains on the advancing 91st, but by July 18 the Division had fought its way through Terriciola, Bagui, Capanneli, Pensacco, and other towns, and had reached the river.

Meanwhile, the 363d Regimental Combat Team, detached from the Division, had swung toward the key port of Leghorn, at the gates of which the Fifth Army had been battering for nearly four weeks. In a surprise thrust, the Powder River men knifed into the city and took it on the 18th. Only two days later elements of the same regiment had advanced to the outskirts of Pisa, and another important objective was about to fall.

In September the Allies in Italy ran into the Germans' Gothic Line, the toughest defensive positions in the Mediterranean. Pillboxes ringed with minefields and wire studded the country-side, and fanatical Nazis fought from within them. Each pill-box had to be knocked out individually, often at hand-grenade range. The peak of Monticelli in particular stood in the way of the 91st, but the Powder River men took the peak and smashed through the Gothic Line in ten days, as riflemen stormed into fortifications so strong 105-millimeter howitzers couldn't breach them. When the 91st took Futa Pass, the Gothic Line became just another line on a tactical map.

Pursuing the enemy from the Arno to Loiano, the 91st was next stopped by the Caesar Line. In October, near Liverguano, the Division fought its bloodiest battle along a rocky cliff almost perpendicular in spots. Flanked on both sides by towering mountains, Doughboys had to sling their weapons and climb with both hands to get at the enemy. That barrier fell on October 13, and then the Division ran into Mt. Adone, a Gibraltar-like obstacle protecting the approaches to Bologna. For six months the 91st fought under its deadly heights, until April 15, 1945, when the Fifth Army launched the attack that spilled out into the Po Valley. The 91st swung over to the Adriatic coast and supported the drive northward of the British Eighth Army. As the Germans in Italy surrendered, the Powder River men were swarming into Trieste.

92nd Infantry Division

THE GERMANS DID A LOT of talking about being the "Master Race." They invented a long list of inferior peoples, conspicuous among whom were Negroes. But that was before the Nazis ran into the 92nd Division. The Buffalo outfit had a few theories of its own, too, including the motto "Deeds Not Words." That turned out to be pretty effective counter-propaganda against the Germans—especially the hundreds of them who were captured by the colored soldiers of the 92nd during its nearly nine months of action on the Italian front.

The 92nd, many of whose officers and all of whose enlisted personnel are Negroes, was activated on October 15, 1942, and among the camps at which it trained was Fort Huachuca, Arizona. There, many years ago, when the American Army was chiefly concerned with Indians, a detachment of colored soldiers was assigned. To keep warm during the cold winter on the prairies, the soldiers killed buffalos and clothed themselves with the hides. The startled Indians began to call them "Black Buffalos," and the 92nd's shoulder patch and nickname carry on the tradition of those early American fighters.

This war's Buffalos embarked for North Africa in June 1944, and soon thereafter were assigned to the Fifth Army front in the Italian Apennines. In September elements of the Division crossed the Arno River and took the city of Lucca. Then the

92nd began to live the usual routine of foot soldiers in that theater—long waits, slow gains, constant patrols, and endless suffering in the cold, bleak hills of central Italy.

The 92nd's first large-scale attack as a division occurred in February 1945, when the Buffalos were given the mission of seizing Monte Cassala, a peak dominating the western coast ports vital to Allied operations. Striking out from along the line of the Fiume–La Force, some three miles south of the stronghold of Massa, the Buffalos stormed the mountain and took it, to the considerable dismay and embarrassment of its Aryan defenders.

During the winter months, the 92nd kept two German divisions tied down in its sector and worked up the Ligurian coast. Not only did it capture the ports of La Spezia and Genoa, but it accomplished the feats so swiftly that the Germans were unable to put into effect plans they had made to render the ports useless when the Allies finally got into them.

From then on, the Division rolled northward, taking Alessandria and Turin on its way. When the war in Italy ended, its accomplishments were summed up by General Mark Clark, commander of the 15th Army Group and better qualified than most other people to appraise the work of the 92nd. In a letter to Major General Edward M. Almond, leader of the Buffalos, General Clark said, "To the 92nd Division went an important assignment in the offensive which ended in unconditional surrender of German forces in Italy. Please convey to your officers and men for me the fact that I value most highly the manner in which that assignment was carried out. We relied upon you to gain ports along the Ligurian coast and you carried out the attack in a most aggressive and successful way. You took La Spezia and then swept on to Genoa, not only taking that great port, but preserving it from terrible bombardment by heavy German guns. With the ports in hand, elements under your command swept into the cities of Alessandria and Turin. These actions played an important part in the victory achieved by the 15th Army Group."

93d Infantry Division

THE FIRST NEGRO OUTFIT larger than a regiment to see combat action in this war was the 93d Infantry Division.

Early in April 1944, the soldiers who wear a French helmet on their shoulders went ashore at Empress Augusta Bay, Bougainville, during the fighting for the Northern Solomons.

And since then they have travelled plenty. They have been in the Treasury Islands; at Morotai, in the Halmahera group of the Netherlands East Indies; and in the Philippines.

Why the French helmet on American insignia? It seems that during World War I the various regiments of the 93d fought not as a division but under different commands in the French Army. Their shoulder patch is the modern reminder of that distant service.

One of the two divisions in our Army whose enlisted personnel is all colored—the other is the 92nd—the 93d fought for a month at Bougainville, working with the 37th Division along the Numa-Numa Trail and the Laruma River. By the end of April the 93d had secured the Saua River and a good deal of territory east of the Torokina River, and had severely inconvenienced the Japs in that area by denying to them a supply route from southern Bougainville.

Late in the spring of 1944, the Division was moved to the Treasury Islands, and, when next disclosed, had leaped the length of New Guinea to Morotai, where it was assigned as a defense force during the early months of 1945. Then the 93d moved on to the Philippines.

94th Infantry Division

THERE WERE DOZENS OF ALLIED DIVISIONS in the European Theater of Operations, but for nearly four months one of them—the 94th Infantry—fought a strange war on a 450-mile front all by itself.

When most of the Germans retreated back across France toward their own borders, after the breakthrough out of Normandy, some of them sought refuge in the ports of the west coast of France. Those at Brest gave up after six weeks of siege, but those at St. Nazaire and Lorient remained a menace. The 94th got the job of keeping them bottled up.

For 111 days the division kept a watchful eye on the 60,000 Germans in the two ports, with frequent battles on the perimeters of the enemy positions. Perhaps one of the oddest roles in the war was that played by the division's cavalry reconnaissance troop, which secretly established itself on an Atlantic island between the two ports, to observe German sea traffic back and forth.

Rarely before had a division operated on so wide a front and with such thinly held lines. To reinforce its own ranks, the 94th trained and equipped 29 battalions of French troops, who later, with the 66th Division, took over many of the division's responsibilities.

The 94th had headed for its "forgotten" war in Brittany right upon landing in Normandy on—coincidentally—D-plus-94, after a stormy crossing of the Channel during which some units were at sea as long as 30 days. For a while the men of the black and gray numerals thought they'd never get to see the main part of the war at all.

But they soon had those illusions shattered. The Dough-boys of the Division—first of all American divisions to have its three principal units designated "Expert Infantry Regiments"—rushed northward from Brittany on New Year's Day, 1945, to help fill the gaps on the Third Army front caused by the shifting of General Patton's forces to help stem Rundstedt's counter-offensive.

Then the 94th ran into the Siegfried Switch Line, a series of strong buffer defenses on the Moselle and east of the Saar River. For the next five weeks the Division fought there, first merely holding ground and then, as the German bulge was lopped off, attacking through the Switch Line with the 10th Armored Division. By erasing this line, the 94th cleared the Saar–Moselle triangle and paved the way for the capture of the key city of Trier.

Then the 94th drove forward and forced a bridgehead across the Saar, at times paddling furiously against a 7-mile-an-hour current which gave the German defenders additional time to hurl steel at the oncoming Doughs. By early in March the Division had consolidated its gains across the Saar and was ready to strike again.

On March 16 the 94th was given the job of spearheading the Third and Seventh Armies' drive to the Rhine. Eight days later, the Division was at the river. It had taken the prize industrial city of Ludwigshafen, had fought for 195 consecutive days, and had captured more than 17,000 prisoners. The "forgotten" Division had made itself well remembered in a war it no longer had to worry about being left out of.

95th Infantry Division

"Give us Der Führer in Berlin—and make it collect!"

That was the command issued to startled German telephone operators by men of the 95th ("Victory") Division following a lightning drive to the Rhine that caught the inhabitants of Rheinhausen, and the Nazi garrison defending it, flat-footed.

They didn't get Hitler on the phone, although the lines to Berlin were still intact, so quickly did the Victorymen strike, but it is a cinch that Adolf had heard of the 95th Division. It was this Division, called the "Bravest of the Brave," which planned and executed one of the most daring maneuvers of the war during the capture of the city of Metz.

Metz was protected by a ring of bristling forts, including Fort Amanvillers, the three Canrobert Forts, and Fort de Feve, east of which spread the intensive Lorraine fortifications. To try to take the city by head-on assault would have been suicide, so the 95th pulled the "hidden ball" trick on the Nazis. It set up a phony front composed of three rifle platoons, one antitank platoon, cooks, clerks, and other regimental headquarters and service company personnel. The small force, using loudspeakers and other means of deception, fooled the Germans into thinking than an entire regiment was fronting the forts. The fake enabled the 378th Regiment to sweep around the northern tip of the fortifications and attack from the rear. Within three hours

Feve was captured. Two hours later the 378th took Some-court. Then Saulny, Vignuelles, Plesnois, and Norroy-le-Veneur tumbled. On the third day of the operation the three Canrobert forts were assaulted and captured. Meanwhile, the 379th Regiment was battering away at Fort Jeanne d'Arc, strong guardian of the western approach to Metz. A bloody battle followed as the outfit smashed through the German main line of resistance and ran wild through seven towns to reach Metz.

In the 14-day battle for Metz the Victorymen killed 1,557 of the enemy, wounded 3,546, and captured 6,082.

The 95th headed for the Saar late in November. and once again pulled a trick that prompted a commendation from the present Secretary of War, Robert P. Patterson. The Victory-men crossed the Saar without the loss of a single man. They crossed in rubber boats. Not a shot was fired. Once across the river, the Doughs of the 95th turned south toward the approach to the main highway bridge over the Saar. It was the only bridge over the Saar in that area, and the 95th needed it intact.

The men took it intact, by once again striking with lightning speed. A radio operator in a German armored car, frantically pounding out a call for help, was bayoneted. A second Kraut, sprinting for the demolition switch on the bridge, was shot dead, five feet short of his goal, by a battalion commander, whose men then hit the bridge and began cutting demolition wires only seven minutes before Nazi engineers were scheduled to blow up the bridge. The advance elements of the 95th found 6,000 pounds of explosives under the bridge.

Guns from every pillbox within range cut loose as the Germans realized what was happening to their prize bridge. But the 95th secured both ends of the crossing, and although it continued to be a hot spot for more than a month, every Doughboy in the Division crossed it.

The battle for the Saarlautern was one of the most vicious of the war. The city's three suburbs across the bridge were integral parts of the Siegfried Line. Massive pillboxes and bunkers were sandwiched between houses, and others cleverly camouflaged as commercial buildings. A battalion objective for an entire day might be a single block, or a part of a block. It was house-to-house, bunker-to-bunker fighting as the men of the

95th encountered mines and booby traps, 88mm. guns firing point-blank. There was a savage hand-to-hand encounter in a ballroom. "There was plenty of dancing there," one of the 95th soldiers said, "but it wasn't a slow foxtrot. It was a dance of death."

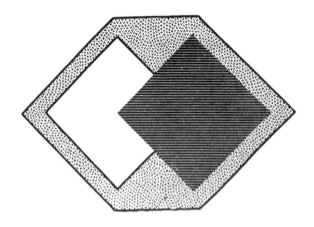

96th Infantry Division

THE 96TH INFANTRY DIVISION wasn't kidding on April Fool's Day. On April 1, 1945, two regiments of the "Deadeye" Division stormed ashore at Okinawa, where for nearly three months the Division was to come up against some of the worst fighting of the whole Pacific war.

Okinawa was the second big campaign for the Deadeyes, who took their nickname because of their marksmanship proficiency during their nearly two years of training in the United States. Activated in August 1942, with a cadre drawn from the 7th Infantry Division, they sailed for Hawaii in July 1944, and continued training there—meeting up with the 7th, back from Attu. On October 20, the 96th entered combat, landing at Leyte in the first hours of General MacArthur's invasion of the Philippines.

The men who wear the overlapping blue and white diamonds, standing, respectively, for courage and purity, helped to liberate Leyte in two months of fighting. Their Division paper, the *Deadeye News*, ran a daily box score of "Good Japs"—dead ones—and by the end of the Leyte campaign the 96th had 7,000 notches on its collective rifle. It had a good collection of Jap souvenirs, too, including one of the largest of any war—a whole Jap cannon collected by four enterprising artillerymen who towed it behind a carabao back to their battery.

Remaining on Leyte during the start of the Luzon operation, the 96th was re-equipped and got set for its next job—Okinawa. Hitting the beaches under Tenth Army command, with its brother Division, the 7th, at its side, as it had been on Leyte, the 96th immediately claimed one distinction when one of its sergeants, racing in 600 yards with a precious bundle on his back, firmly implanted the first American flag on the soil of the Ryukyus.

Then came weeks of steady fighting against fanatical resistance from Japs who had to be burned and dug out of hidden caves. The Deadeyes swarmed over Tombstone Ridge, and, in mid-May, hit their hardest opposition at Conical Hill, overlooking the Yonabaru Airfield. When the 96th took Conical Hill, on May 14, it deprived the Japs of their last good observation point on Okinawa. Then the Division gobbled up the airfield. A month later, the Deadeyes cracked the center of the Jap southern defense line by taking Yaeju Hill and pushed on to the south. Just a day before the official end of the campaign, which was announced on June 20, the assistant commander of the 96th, Brigadier General Claudius M. Easley, was killed in action. A crack shot himself, he had had much to do with the sharpshooting of the rest of the Deadeyes—men like Private First Class Clarence Craft, who won nationwide fame for killing 30 of the enemy during his first combat action, and breaking a stalemate that had held up two regiments for ten days.

Seven thousand dead Japs had seemed like a substantial number on Leyte, but by the time the *Deadeye News* got around to printing box scores at the end of the Okinawa campaign the figure had been left far behind. By then, the Deadeyes' collection of "good" Japs had reached the impressive total of 20,000.

97th Infantry Division

SIX MONTHS BEFORE V-E DAY, it looked very much to the men of the "Trident" Division as if their first war action would be against the Japanese. At that time the Division, which had been activated in February 1943, was stationed in California, with its training all completed and its men ready for battle. But in the Army plans can change quickly, even plans involving the 14,000 men and hundreds of vehicles of a division. Just two years after its activation, in February 1945, the 97th sailed for the European Theater of Operations.

In the complicated design of the 97th's shoulder patch, the three prongs of the trident represent the states from which the personnel of the outfit were originally drawn—Maine, Vermont, and New Hampshire. Neptune's trident was selected as an appropriate symbol since Maine and New Hampshire touch the Atlantic Ocean. The blue of the shield stands for the freshwater lakes of New England, the white of the border for the snow-covered mountains of the region.

The 97th landed in France at Le Havre, and was first assigned to the Fifteenth Army. Held in reserve for several weeks, the Division then marched from France to Belgium and on into Germany, where it was assigned to the First Army and thrown into action near Düsseldorf during operations to liquidate the Germans trapped in the Ruhr pocket. After only a few days in that area, the Division was moved down along the Rhine to Bonn, at the southern end of the pocket. On April 3, the 97th crossed the Rhine, and then went back into action along the Sieg River, capturing Siegburg and several other German towns. Patrols of the 97th frequently sneaked across the Sieg during this fighting in canvas boats. Then the Division began to move back toward Düsseldorf again, to close the pocket from the south.

During the final mopping-up operations in the pocket, the 97th took thousands of prisoners. Then it was transferred to the Third Army, was shifted to General Patton's front, and was committed to action again near the town of Hof. The 97th remained in battle for five weeks, moving up with the Third Army into Czechoslovakia.

At a point near the Czechoslovakian city of Luditz, patrols from the Division met up with elements of the Russian Army. After V-E Day, the Division was moved back into Germany, and then prepared to sail back to the United States for redeployment to the Pacific. And in the fall, finally, the Division that had expected to begin its travels in Jap-held territory found itself in Japan, as one of the two Divisions—the 86th was the other—that actually got redeployed from Europe.

98th Infantry Division

THE 98TH INFANTRY DIVISION never got to fire a shot in combat, but it wasn't for any lack of desire. The luck of war kept the division stationed in Hawaii from the time it went overseas—April 1944—until the Japanese surrendered sixteen months later.

But the 98th got a look at the enemy, if only at an enemy already defeated. The "Iroquois" Division was one of the Divisions selected for occupation duty in the home islands of Japan.

The Indian Chief shoulder patch of the 98th Division has a long history behind it. The Division, between World Wars, was kept alive as a Reserve outfit by the New York officers who had served in World War I, and their insignia reflects their geographical origins. New York was the home of the old Iroquois Confederacy, composed of five Indian nations, and the five feathers on the Chief's head symbolize this ancient government.

Blue and orange was selected as the divisional colors because they had earlier been the colors of the Netherlands House of Nassau, which sent its colonists to New York.

The Chief himself? The Iroquois men of today identify him as Hiawatha.

99th Infantry Division

THE CAPTURE, INTACT, OF THE Remagen Bridge, was one of the major turning points in the Allied victory over the Nazi war machine.

The men who achieved it have been praised in all languages except the German and Japanese, and rightfully so.

But the men who held the Remagen bridgehead, against the most savage counterattacks, have been slightly neglected, and wrongfully so.

The men of the 99th Infantry Division, who wear the blue and white squares, taken from the coat of arms of William Pitt, on their shoulder patch, were among those who denied the Nazis' efforts to re-take the vital bridgehead.

They went into this battle without much combat hardening, but they held their ground. The black background of their patch, representing the steel of Pennsylvania, was rightfully chosen.

After fighting out of the Remagen bridgehead, the GIs of the "Checkerboard" Division captured scores of German cities and towns. The Germans were in full rout, and the 99th exploited this advantage with a drive of blitz proportions. They never gave the Nazis a chance to take a breather, to reorganize. One prisoner told the Division's G-2 that he hadn't seen an officer in a week, and had no idea of where the main body of his unit had gone. The 99th moved so fast in this drive that it was not unusual for the division headquarters to move forward each day.

It was the 99th which, after crossing the Wied River, sped in double columns down the super highway to capture Limburg, communications center on the Lahn River. The Lahn, with Limburg as its hub, was the last natural water barrier between the First and Third Armies, east of the Rhine.

Joining the Third Army's push toward Austria, the 99th bore down on Ingolstadt and captured a Panzer Lehr (training) division, whose strength had been cut from 10,000 to 3,000.

The Checkerboards were on the offensive for 24 days in March, capturing 200 German towns and overrunning 495 square miles of enemy territory.

At the war's end the 99th was deep in Germany at Warzburg. Its record showed that it crossed not only the Rhine, but the Erft Canal, Wied and Dill Rivers, and many minor tributaries as well.

The Checkerboards got their first combat in Belgium in November 1944, when they relieved the 9th Infantry Division and 102nd Cavalry Group, and engaged in a rousing artillery battle with the Nazis near Wirtzfeld. A month later they aided in the defense of the V Corps sector north of the Roer River. The Checkerboards were in the midst of a fierce armored fight during the push on Elsenborn at the start of the year. After taking Elsenborn, the 99th drove on to capture Berg, and then prepared itself for the push into Germany. In March, the Division started a surge that drove it into the Reich at Aachen. It then swept past Düren and Jülich, turned north at Düsseldorf, back down to the southeast to Remagen, and from there across the Rhine.

100th Infantry Division

ON THE FIRST CELEBRATION OF INFANTRY DAY, June 15, 1944, a battalion of the "Century" Division marched smartly through the streets of New York City. It was an impressive parade, and the men of the 100th were glad that they had been singled out to put on the show. It wasn't their first distinction, either. A few weeks before that, one of them, a technical sergeant, had been picked as the first recipient of the Expert Infantryman Badge.

But the 100th still wasn't too happy. Nine days before, thousands of Infantrymen like themselves had stormed the beaches of Normandy, and the Century Division was still a parade-ground outfit in the States.

A year later the story was different.

Resting in Europe after V-E Day, the 100th could look back on a distinguished combat record of its own. The technical sergeant who had had a badge pinned on him by Lieutenant General Lesley J. McNair had turned it in for a better one—the Combat Infantryman Badge. And he wasn't a technical sergeant any more; he had won a battlefield commission. And on many a shirt that had been plain in New York's parade was pinned a Purple Heart.

The Century Division landed in Southern France on October 20, two months after the Allied invasion from the Mediterranean. The three veteran infantry divisions that made that landing—the 3d, 36th, and 45th—had had little rest in many months of battle, and the 100th was rushed up to the line. Eleven days after it reached the European continent it relieved elements of the 45th on the Seventh Army front, south of the Meurthe River in eastern France.

Crossing the Meurthe at Baccarat, the Division captured an important German supply base at Raon-l'Etape, and, ripping through the German defensive positions in the lower Vosges Mountains, took Moyenmontier, Senones, and St. Blaise. By seizing and holding Schirmeck, the 100th prevented the enemy from moving down through the Bruche River Valley and endangering the subsequent Seventh Army drive into Alsace and to the city of Strasbourg.

As winter came on, the Centurymen swung north toward the Maginot Line. At the south end of the line, the most heavily fortified point was the town of Bitche, protected by the stronghold of Fort Schiesseck. On its way to Bitche, the 100th encountered fanatical opposition from the Germans, and when it got there, it found itself up against a series of four-foot concrete emplacements and numerous blockhouses, all backed up by thundering batteries of German artillery. Fort Schiesseck itself, a bare ridge dotted with blockhouses, was a tough nut to crack, but the Century division reduced it despite direct hits from German 88s on advancing Infantry units, despite hard, snow-covered ground, and despite a seemingly endless series of fierce enemy counterattacks.

When it was all over, the 100th received high praise from General Jacob L. Devers, 6th Army Group commander. "Your great accomplishments," he said, "forced the enemy to give up the offensive action on your front."

Afterwards, the 100th assisted materially in cleaning up the enemy forces in the huge Saarland pocket between the Third and Seventh Armies. On the second celebration of Infantry Day, it could look back on a hard job well done.

101st Airborne Division

SURROUNDED AT BASTOGNE, cut off from all supplies, and with tremendous forces of Nazi "supermen" closing in for the kill, the 101st Airborne Division was asked to surrender.

"Nuts!" was the answer of the 101st's acting commander, Brigadier General Anthony C. McAuliffe.

"Nuts!" echoed his men, thus giving to American military tradition a slogan that will live forever with such battle cries as "Don't give up the ship!" "I have just begun to fight!" and "Do you . . . want to live forever?"

For this heroic action—an action that more than any other blunted Rundstedt's mighty winter offensive against the Allied forces—the whole 101st was awarded the Distinguished Unit Citation.

The men who wear the screaming eagle on their shoulders are many-sided. They're rough, tough, unyielding, in battle. But it was the 101st men who held the first full-scale art exhibit in liberated Europe. In their drive across France, and then into Nazidom up to and including Berchtesgaden, they captured a cache of priceless paintings, stolen from the Louvre and other museums by Hermann Goering and his cohorts. The works of art were tastefully arranged, lighted, and beyond a sign proclaiming that the display was by courtesy of the 101st Airborne, GIs were invited to gaze upon millions of dollars' worth of art treasures. Paratroopers who had withstood the fiercest Nazi attacks at Bastogne acted as guides and instructors during the art exhibit.

It was the men of the 101st who captured two of the most notorious Nazi fanatics. They first put the irons on Robert Ley, leader of the Nazi labor party, and one of Hitler's leading councilmen. Their second—and biggest—bag, was Julius Streicher, the infamous perpetrator of racial hatred, under whose orders thousands of Jews were scourged and killed.

The 101st, after a long period of training in England, made its D-Day landing in France without major loss, and began its march across Normandy. Strong resistance was met near Ste.Marie-du-Mont, but the Division fought its way through to Carentan, a vital German stronghold.

In December the 101st was rushed to Bastogne in trucks. Hold. Hold. Hold. No matter what. That was its orders. At the finish of the Bastogne battle General McAuliffe said of his officers and men: "With the type of soldier I had under my command, possessing such fighting spirit, all that I had to do was to make a few basic decisions—my men did the rest."

A British corps commander, near the end of the Holland campaign, told Screaming Eagle soldiers: "I have commanded four corps during my army career, but the 101st Airborne Division is the fightingest outfit I ever had under my command."

Where did the 101st get its Screaming Eagle shoulder patch?

It goes back to the Civil War and the "Iron Brigade," one regiment of which possessed the famous war eagle, "Old Abe." A sergeant carried him into the smoke and fire of a civil war battle and the eagle, perched on a shield between the national color and the regimental color, screamed above the roar of the guns. The eagle, it is said, went through 36 battles, being wounded at Vicksburg and again at Corinth. During the battle of Corinth, the men of the 101st will tell you, a Confederate general offered a substantial reward for the bird's capture or death.

But he didn't have to pay off.

The eagle of the 101st screamed defiance at the enemy many times in World War II.

102nd Infantry Division

THE DOUGHBOYS' DREAM—a ringside seat at a decisive battle, with someone else doing the fighting—came true to the foot-sloggers of the 102nd Infantry Division.

One of the last battles fought in Germany, just before the unconditional surrender of the Nazi war machine, was fought near Tangermünde, and the men who call themselves the Ozarks, and who wear an O and a Z on their shoulder patch to prove they aren't fooling, were witnesses, not participants.

The battle was fought between the Russians advancing on the Elbe River, and the Nazis who were trying to get across the river to surrender to the men of the 102nd.

The fire fight went on for hours, but the Ozarks didn't dare join in—even if they had craved another chance at combat—for fear of hitting the Russians. So, they just took it easy on their bank of the river, and watched the Reds and the Nazis slug it out.

The Germans finally managed to cross the Elbe, cutting through thousands of civilians who were retreating in face of the onrushing Reds, to lay down their arms to the 102d. They then boasted of their cleverness in escaping the Russians. These German soldiers, craven quitters, were the last elements of the once mighty German Ninth and Twelfth Armies.

The Ozarks went overseas in September 1944, but did not see action until near the end of the year. Serving under the Ninth Army, the Ozarks entered combat near the Roer River, taking Lovenich, and then fighting in the München-Gladbach area. Late in February 1945, the Ozark Doughs spearheaded the Ninth's crossing of the Roer, and then attacked north, toward the Rhine. In their dash to the Rhine, the "Hillbillies," as they do not mind being called, overran 86 towns and cities.

One of the most important spots to fall to the 102nd was Krefeld, a key railroad and communications center. At this city the Division stored its supplies in caves that the Romans had used centuries before as barracks, and, when taken by the Yanks, were the site of a tremendous rocket factory.

The Ozarks chased the Germans from the Rhine to the Elbe, and, on reaching the Elbe north of Magdeburg, did extensive patrol duty while awaiting the arrival of the Russians. On May 4, the German Ninth and Eleventh Armies surrendered to the 102nd at Worgl. The Division was at this town on V-E Day.

103d Infantry Division

FOR MANY MONTHS, the Allied forces in Italy struggled slowly toward a junction with the Seventh Army, fighting on the southern flank of General Eisenhower's forces on the Western Front. Finally, just before V-E Day, two American units met in Italy, south of the Brenner Pass—the Fifth Army's 88th Division, and the Seventh's 103rd.

The soldiers who wear a giant cactus on their shoulders had driven down through the pass where Hitler and Mussolini had connived. The "Cactus" Division had come from a triumphant entry into Innsbruck, capital of the Austrian Tyrol, which had been taken by the 409th Infantry Regiment to the accompaniment of a wild ovation from the Tyrolese.

But it wasn't all glory and cheers for the 103rd.

They had some hard battles starting on November 9, when they went into combat and helped the VI Corps of the Seventh Army launch its attack through the Vosges Mountains. The Cactusmen, after crossing a river and taking a key hill dominating St. Dié, had cracked through the mountain and 14 days later, spilled out into plains beyond. And one of their units, Company I of the 411th Infantry, had staked a claim to being the first Seventh Army outfit to touch German soil, when it fought its way into Wissenbourg.

In December and January, the Germans counterattacked, just as they were doing in the Ardennes up north, and the 103rd saw hard fighting as it helped to stem the enemy tide. On January 25 and 26, the Cactusmen were conspicuous in crushing a German salient at Schillersdorf, as the Nazis made their final all-out bid to retake Alsace.

A little later, the Division crossed the Palatinate border at the same spot the Seventh Army had occupied three months earlier, before the German counteroffensive had forced it to withdraw temporarily. Then, in the rugged Hardt Mountains, the 103rd took on some of the toughest enemy positions, and crawled successfully past the concrete pillboxes the Germans had installed to defend the area.

After its junction with the Fifth Army, the 103rd returned to Innsbruck and went on guard duty there. When the war ended, the Cactus Division organized sight-seeing tours for its soldiers who had already traveled so far. One private first class was asked for his opinion of these tours, and his answer might have been made by any GI in Europe. "I'd like to see some of the places I went through on the double with my nose in dirt," he said.

104th Infantry Division

"NOTHING IN HELL MUST STOP THE TIMBERWOLVES" is the slogan of the 104th Division. Nothing in Germany did. From the moment it went into action as part of the Canadian First Army in Belgium on October 23, 1944, the "Timberwolf" Division compiled an impressive record of wartime achievements. Under the command of Major General Terry de la M. Allen, already famous for his leadership of the 1st Infantry Division in North Africa, the 104th had scarcely arrived in Europe when it began to make news, by its realistic training in forward areas which had been cleared of the enemy only a short time before. In Holland, the Division spearheaded the drive of the British I Corps across the Mark River and to the Maas River. Both British and Canadian forces expressed official admiration of the courage and enthusiasm of the Timberwolves.

Moving over to the American First Army front, the 104th relieved the 1st Infantry Division at Aachen and, on November 16, jumped off toward the Roer River. In ensuing battles, it distinguished itself by the effectiveness of its night operations. It surprised its own superiors by the speed with which it conquered the great industrial cities of Eschweiler, Weisweiler, and Stolberg, prompting Lieutenant General J. Lawton Collins, commander of the VII Corps, to pay tribute to the "leadership, dash and sound training of the division."

On its way to the Roer, the 104th forced a crossing of the

Inde River, in a brilliant series of night attacks that confused the Germans and upset their defensive plans. In a few days, the Timberwolves had cleared the entire sector assigned to them between the Inde and the Roer, and had won further credit for themselves by their skill in taking Lammersdorf, Inden, and Lucherberg.

During Rundstedt's breakthrough, the 104th occupied a defensive sector on the Roer, opposite Düren, remaining there until nearly the end of February, with the principal mission of preventing the Germans from advancing again in Aachen. That job completed, the Division headed toward Cologne, seizing Düren and Huchem-Stammeln on the way, and taking their main objective on March 7. Once again the Timberwolves' prowess at night featured their progress.

Fifteen days later, the 104th crossed the Rhine at the Remagen Bridgehead, and in nine days advanced a total of 193 miles east and north, ending up at Paderborn. Linking up with the 3d Armored Division there, the 104th halted briefly and then started off on another quick advance, this time covering 175 miles in 15 days and culminating at the Mulde River. On its way the 104th crossed the Weser and Saale Rivers, and captured Halle, Bitterfeld and Delitzsch.

Finally, just before V-E Day, the 104th linked up with the Russians along the Elbe River.

106th Infantry Division

SEVERAL WEEKS AFTER V-E DAY, it was announced from Europe that the 106th Infantry Division had been assigned the job of guarding thousands of German prisoners of war. No outfit had a better right to claim that job than the "Golden Lion" Division, for the 106th, in the war's major setback for the Allies in Europe, had more of its men captured than any other American division.

The story began in mid-December, when the 106th, which had left the United States only two months before, was moved up toward the front and—because it was without any previous combat experience—assigned to a supposedly relatively quiet sector in the Ardennes.

Then it happened. Rundstedt, who had secretly been planning an all-out counteroffensive, gave the word, and the massed might of the German armies smashed into the American lines. There is always one point at which the attack is heaviest—and that was the point at which the 106th was stationed.

The 106th was deployed along a rocky, wooded ridge called Schnee Eifel, near the city of St.Vith, with its men scattered along a 27-mile front. In the foggy dawn of December 16 the Germans began their attack, with a tremendous artillery barrage. The pro-Nazi residents of St.Vith, tipped off in advance, had scurried into their cellars, and the fury of the German barrage crashed into the positions of the 106th. Then came the enemy tanks and the enemy infantry, and, along with them, English-speaking German soldiers disguised in captured American MP uniforms, to add confusion to the scene.

For two ghastly days, the 106th fought back, though vastly outnumbered by the oncoming enemy. The 422nd and 423rd Infantry regiments held out as long as they could, without food, water, or ammunition, and finally sent through a last radio message that they were destroying their equipment. Then there was silence. The remaining regiment of the division, the 424th, hung on grimly near St.Vith, and helped to keep the Germans from overrunning that vital communications center.

When the 106th's casualties were added up, it had lost 8,663 men, some 7,000 of whom were prisoners.

But the Golden Lion wasn't licked yet. Moved to the rear to re-organize, and with its ranks filled with replacements, it stormed back into the Battle of the Bulge in January and stayed in action till the counteroffensive had been crushed. Later it took up the fight on the south flank of the First Army's sector in the Siegfried Line, and in March it was pulled back again, this time to Rennes, and held in reserve.

As German resistance began to crumble from north to south, the 106th was brought back toward the lines to help cope with the terrific problem caused by the thousands of prisoners falling into Allied hands. By the middle of June, the Golden Lions had control over 16 prisoner-of-war enclosures with 910,000 inhabitants—more than 15 times the total number of Germans taken by the AEF during World War I. Ardennes had been avenged.

Americal Division

THE AMERICAL DIVISION is not the American Division.

Americal is not the nickname of a division; it is its name.

And the men who wear the Southern Cross shoulder patch of our Army's only active unnumbered division would rather you didn't forget it.

When the war started there was no Americal Division, and none was contemplated. But there were a lot of Japs on the rampage in the Southwest Pacific, and as part of the Allied plan to throttle any hopes they might entertain of invading Australia and the islands immediately off its coast, Task Force 6814 was rushed to Australia and then over to New Caledonia. Troops trained for action on the decks of their ships.

The Japs never dared hit Australia, or New Caledonia, either, but Task Force 6814 wasn't through. Its defensive mission accomplished, it began to prepare for the attack. Its various units were organized into a regular infantry division, under Major General Alexander M. Patch, who was later promoted to command of the Seventh Army on the other side of the world. Its name—derived from a combination of America and New Caledonia—was invented by a sergeant in its ranks.

Its deeds spoke for themselves.

The story began in October 1942, two months after the 1st Marine Division landed on Guadalcanal. Sent in to relieve the Marines, the Americal found that there was still plenty of Jap resistance. Henderson Field was firmly in our hands, but from the nearby heights of Mount Austen, the Japs had excellent observation on the vital airfield. The hill had to be taken, and on December 17 the America's 132nd Infantry set out to do the job. Seven times the Doughboys charged up, and seven times Japs of the crack Oka Regiment counterattacked. But finally the Japs were washed out, and they lost all interest in Henderson Field. For actions like that, some elements of the American were rewarded by the Navy with its Presidential Unit Citation— the only Army units to be thus honored.

Fighting on Guadalcanal lasted until February 1943, and the American moved to the Fiji Islands for defense of that area and further combat training. Once again no Japs dared come near them, and once again they set off on an offensive mission when, in December 1943, they joined the fight at Bougainville. On Christmas Day, the American went into the line. It stayed on Bougainville for nearly a year, battling the Japanese in thick jungle on the edges of an American perimeter beyond which thousands of enemy soldiers waited, suicidally throwing themselves again and again at our positions. By the time the American was relieved there, on December 10, 1944, it had established itself as a veteran, jungle-wise outfit.

Its experience came in handy. It was transported north to the Philippines, where General MacArthur's forces had landed on Leyte late in October. In less than five months, American units saw action on no less than thirteen Philippine islands. After mopping up on Leyte and Samar, the men who wore the Southern Cross landed on the small islands of Ticao, Burias, Biri, Capul, Poro, Mactan, Cauit and Olongapo, and hit the major islands of Bohol, Negros and Cebu. The men who had started out without a name and who ended up without a number had done all right.

Philippine Division

YOU DIDN'T SEE MANY SOLDIERS around during most of the war with the carabao of the Philippine Division on their shoulders. Everybody knows why their insignia were so little on public exhibition. They were among the defenders of Bataan.

The Philippine Division was a Regular Army outfit stationed in the Philippine Islands, and composed of Regulars on tours of duty in that area.

When the Japanese struck in December 1941, the Division, along with thousands of Filipinos put under arms for the defense of their homeland, and also existing units of the native-born Philippine Scouts, tried gallantly to halt the inexorable enemy surge.

General Jonathan M. Wainwright, a former commander of the Philippine Division, knew what the trained soldiers of the outfit could do under normal conditions, but he never realized to what heights of gallantry they would rise in spite of hopelessly inadequate food, ammunition, and medical supplies. They just wouldn't give up.

These were the men of the foxholes of Bataan. Their division was the first to engage in battle with the land armies of one of our enemies in World War II.

They knew the terrible cost and the agony of defeat.

They hoped in vain for the help their country was not yet able to send.

They fought when no one could have blamed them for surrendering.

They were cited three times for their heroism.

When they finally had to quit, those who were still alive suffered the tortures and indignities of the Death March and long years in filthy Japanese prison camps.

Their division ceased to exist as an active Army unit. Its men were gone, its records were gone—everything but its spirit was gone.

Now a few of those men are back home again. They wear their shoulder patch with pride, too, but perhaps with the special pride of men who have tasted all the worst of war.

1st Cavalry Division

THE 1ST CAVALRY DIVISION and the 37th Infantry Division staged one of the hottest competitive races in modern warfare for the honor of being the first to reach the city of Manila.

The race started at Lingayen Gulf, and the 1st Cavalry won by a few hours, thanks to a final all-out blitz that carried it 114 miles in 60 hours. By being the first troops to reach the capital of the Philippines the 1st avenged General Jonathan M. Wainwright, courageous defender of Corregidor and Bataan, and a former brigade commander of the division.

One of the "Hell for Leather" Division's first orders in Manila was to punch forward, at any cost, and relieve the some 4,000 civilian internees in Santo Tomás University. In a spectacular dash through the barricaded, burning city, and with the enemy defending from every house and building, the 1st, with Sherman tanks as a spearhead, overwhelmed the Japanese garrison at the University and liberated the near-starved internees.

The 4,000 prisoners, most of them American citizens, never will forget the shoulder patch of the 1st—a large shield of Cavalry color, yellow, with black diagonal bar and horse's head in upper right hand corner. The bar signifies the division as first in name and battle.

Dismounted early in 1942, the 1st Cavalry Division landed in Australia in July of 1943, and for months slaved at amphibious training and jungle fighting methods. It was a hard-hitting Doughboy outfit, ready to carry on the tradition of successes that elements of the division had started in the Civil and Indian wars, when it invaded the Admiralty Islands in February 1944. The Division landed on Los Negros Island and, despite intense opposition from the Japanese, swept inland to seize and secure Momote airstrip within half an hour. It also captured Manus Island, later to be transformed into one of the Navy's great Pacific bases.

The Division next went into combat in the bloody battle for Leyte. For its action there, against the finest Japanese combat divisions, the Division was cited. The former horsemen, who dote on speed of attack, established a near record when, within five hours after hitting the beach, they took the heavily defended Cataisan airfield, and, a day after landing, captured Taclobán, capital of Leyte. Also, they took the nearby island of Samar.

No Doughboy outfit ever fought with greater courage and stamina than did the 1st when it was given the mean task of securing and holding the mountainous country separating Ormoc and Leyte valleys. For 42 days of the monsoon season the men endured what General Walter Krueger described as "the most brutal terrain and conditions American soldiers have ever been asked to stand." The rainfall was torrential, and often it rode on the wings of gales that reached 80 miles per hour. They sweated it out during the day and near froze at night. Food, ammunition, and medical supplies had to be brought in by air drop, by native carrier trains, and by carabao pack. They fought their way up trails knee-deep in mud, waded neck-deep jungle streams, while under almost constant artillery, mortar and small-arms fire. There was much hand-to-hand work with the fanatical Japs, and on several occasions cooks, engineers, signal, and quartermaster units were used in the line. For each of its own soldiers killed on Leyte, the 1st accounted for 24 of the enemy.

The 1st Cavalry Division is rough, tough and rugged, and proud of it. But it is equally proud of being just about the most spit-and-polish outfit of them all. There is a saying in the South Pacific that when you see an MP, up to his waist in mud, but with shined shoes and wearing white gloves, you know you are close to the 1st Cavalry Division.

Armored Insignia

ALL SOLDIERS ASSIGNED TO ARMORED UNITS wear shoulder insignia of the same basic design. The triangular patch's three colors signify the three arms of the service which were merged to form our armored forces: blue for Infantry, red for Field Artillery, and yellow for Cavalry.

The superimposed tank tread, cannon, and thunderbolt represent the mobility, power and speed of armor.

Soldiers assigned to non-tactical armored organizations, such as the Armored Center and the Armored Replacement Training Center, wear the plain triangular patch without numerical embellishment. Armored Corps are designated by the appropriate Roman numeral. Insignia of our 16 armored divisions bear the Arabic numeral appropriate to each one.

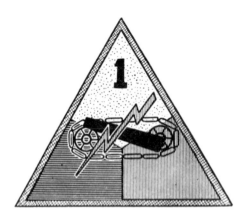

1st Armored Division

IN THE CLOSING MONTHS OF THE TITANIC STRUGGLE that drove Germany to its knees, there were countless references to the part played by American armor in the victory drive across Naziland.

Yet, the outfit that probably contributed more than any other to the success of our armor wasn't even in Germany—it was down in northern Italy slugging it out with the Nazis there.

To the 1st Armored, the "Old Ironsides" Division, rightfully belongs much of the credit for the battle brilliance of American armor. It could just as well be called the "Guinea Pig" Division. For it was one of the first, and for a long time the only, American armored outfit in action. It learned on the battlefields of North Africa and Anzio lessons that were taught its sister units prior to combat, so they didn't have to learn the hard and bloody way.

In the North African campaign, where it was often on the defensive, the 1st learned the necessity of tank-infantry cooperation and coordination, and in every period out of the line it spread that gospel, perfecting teamwork.

The lessons the 1st learned in the classrooms of Oran, Mateur, Faïd Pass, Kasserine Pass, Cassino, and Anzio, became chapters in the textbooks studied at Fort Knox, Kentucky, home of the Armored Center and the Armored Replacement Training Center.

There is scarcely a type of terrain, except jungle, over which the 1st Armored Division has not fought. It swirled through the sand of the Tunisian desert, plowed through the Pontine marshes below Rome, churned through the mountains in the Apennines campaign, and slashed along the plains of the Po Valley.

The 1st Armored sailed for Northern Ireland in April 1942, and trained there for many months under the guidance of British tankmen who had faced the Nazi blitzkrieg in Holland, Belgium, and France. The 1st Armored had its first taste of combat when it went ashore at Oran at the start of the historic North Africa campaign. The Oran plan was a simple one—a pincers movement from both sides to pinch off the city and airfields on the outskirts, while troop-laden destroyers crashed the boom across the harbor to capture the dock area and save port installations from destruction. It was a brief battle, but the 1st Armored made its first down payment in human life. An entire battalion of its Armored Infantry was lost when shore lights spotted the destroyers charging the harbor and shore guns sank them.

Soon afterward, the 1st Armored Division was attached to the famous British Eighth Army, and there was hardly a major engagement in which the men of Old Ironsides failed to take part. They fought at Maknassy, El Guettar, and Faïd Pass, but not as a division. The battle for Tunisia had reached a critical stage before the 1st got its first chance to operate as a whole. The 1st Armored held Mateur. After what was known as the "Battle of the Mousetrap" the Division, in three days of swift, stabbing action slashed clear across to the Mediterranean at Porto Farina. The flying columns of the 1st Armored avenging the mauling it had taken earlier at Kasserine Pass, chopped the opposition to bits and took 23,000 prisoners.

After action before Cassino, the 1st Armored Division was shifted to Anzio in the maneuver that was designed to turn the flank of the Gustav Line and force the Nazis to retire from Cassino. For four months, as the 93-square mile Allied toehold absorbed every bit of punishment that the Germans could throw at it, the 1st Armored was there, a mobile reserve, plugging holes when it seemed the Germans must break through and drive our forces into the sea. When it wasn't fighting, the Division was in training, preparing for the day of the breakthrough. The 1st's training area was so close to the front lines that the Germans could see the maneuvers through binoculars and plaster the tanks with artillery fire.

When the race for Rome began the 1st Armored Division was in the lead. The men of the 1st Armored swear that it was their reconnaissance squadron that was first into Rome. They have the word of Rome's chief of police, whom they captured, that there were no other Allied troops in the city when the forward elements of the Division slipped in. The 1st Armored didn't stay around Rome to enjoy the sights. Five days after the fall of the Eternal City, the division was 200 miles north, chasing remnants of the Hermann Goering Panzers.

Before Bologna, the whole Division left its vehicles and fought on foot as Infantrymen. It took Milan. It split northern Italy in two by racing through to the Swiss border at Como. When the war ended it was headed for Austria.

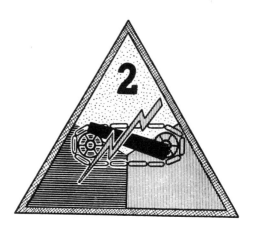

2nd Armored Division

In November 1942, when the Allies landed in North Africa, the ultimate goal of every unit and every soldier in the invasion was Berlin. In the Western Assault Force that had the job of taking Casablanca, back then, was part of the 2nd Armored Division— the outfit that, in later fighting in Sicily, France, Belgium, Holland and Germany, fully established its right to the proud name "Hell on Wheels." And when the American Army began rolling into Berlin, 32 months after the African landings, the 2d Armored rode at the head of the procession, our first division to enter the enemy capital.

After French resistance ceased in North Africa, the 2nd Armored trained with the Fifth Army along the Spanish Morocco frontier. Elements of the division took part in the Tunisian fighting, in conjunction with the 1st Armored. In July 1943, Hell on Wheels struck again, this time at Gela, Sicily. The twisting trails of that mountainous island didn't provide the sort of terrain conditions the tankers were used to, and were a far cry from the flat plains of North Africa. But the 2nd Armored nonetheless contributed materially to the quick defeat of the enemy, fighting at Campobello, Palermo, and other hot spots.

While the 1st Armored moved into Italy with the Fifth Army, the other of these two veteran tank units was shifted back to England to train for the invasion of France. Early in June 1944,

Hell on Wheels charged into Normandy. Its powerful machines roamed far and wide across the European countryside, striking into France, Germany, Holland and Belgium. On June 12, 1945, the whole outfit was awarded the Belgian Croix de Guerre—marking the first time that Belgium had ever conferred that decoration on a foreign division.

The 2d Armored Division liked to be where the fighting was tough, and when the Germans broke through the American lines in the Ardennes counteroffensive, that was where the 2d Armored went. When the First Army rallied from the blow and began to turn back the enemy threat, the American attack on the north flank of the Nazi bulge was spearheaded by the tanks and men of Hell on Wheels.

For the dash from the Rhine to the Elbe early in the spring, the 2d Armored was transferred to the Ninth Army. It reached the Elbe ahead of all other American units, and was ready to plunge across and sail straight into Berlin, when its fierce dash toward the city was halted by orders from higher headquarters.

The Russians, of course, got to Berlin first, but no 2d Armored man will ever admit that he couldn't have been there sooner if he'd been given a free rein. So it was only the military equivalent of poetic justice that, when the citizens of Berlin finally got their first glimpse of American armed might, they saw Hell on Wheels.

3d Armored Division

YOU WILL NEVER HAVE ANY TROUBLE addressing a soldier of the 3d Armored Division.

"Call me Spearhead" is his favorite phrase.

The speedy outfit that led the First Army out of Normandy and across France, closed the Falaise Gap, crashed the Siegfried Line, and took Cologne, claimed a lot of "firsts" for itself. It even announced that one of its men was first to swim in the Rhine.

The Spearhead Division liked to be out front, and that led to tragedy in Germany when its own commander, Major General Maurice Rose, got out in front of even his own men, was captured by a German tank, and was killed by the tank commander during the surrender.

From the breakthrough west of St.Lô to the final surrender of the Nazis, the 3d Armored was in the thick of things. After unwieldy tank fighting in the hedgerows, the Spearhead broke out at Marigny, with the 1st Infantry Division, and headed due south to Mayenne. In mid-August, the 3d Armored was ordered to close the Falaise-Argentan pocket in which the German Seventh Army was caught, and the Division finished the job near Putanges on August 18. By August 24, the Spearhead had rolled through Courville and Chartres and was poised at the banks of the Seine.

The next evening the 3d Armored began to jump the river, and, once over, it began a mad dash across France that brought it clear up to the Siegfried Line in just 18 days. Soissons, Mons, Namur, and Liège were among the dozens of places in the swath cut by the Spearhead. At Mons alone, the 3d Armored cut off 40,000 Germans and captured three generals among 8,000 prisoners. And then the Spearhead set forth on the first invasion of Germany since the days of Napoleon:

September 10: It fired the first American artillery shell to land on German soil.

September 12: It became the first unit to pass the German border.

September 13: It became the first to take a German town (Roetgen) and first to breach the Siegfried Line.

September 15: It became the first division completely to pierce the Siegfried Line.

September 18 (as the final touch): Its antiaircraft gunners became the first Americans to shoot down a German plane from German soil.

Driving on, the Spearhead was halted only by the Ardennes counteroffensive, when it swung into the fray near Houffalize and cut an important highway leading to St. Vith.

The 3d Armored Division took Cologne and Paderborn, helped the 2d Armored shut tight the back door to the Ruhr, crossed the Saale, and, with other American units converging on Berlin, raced to the Elbe near Dessau, where it saw its last action. It had many an achievement behind it: the liberation of political prisoners of the Gestapo from a prison at Cologne, the seizure of a trainload of V-2s near Bromskirchen, and even the surrender of a weird band of 200 members of the Hitler Jugend, led by a 16-year-old boy, who formally handed over their weapons (small-sized dress daggers) to representatives of the 3d Armored at the end of the war.

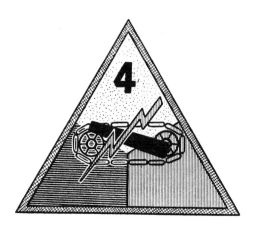

4th Armored Division

FROM THE DAY IT WAS ACTIVATED, the 4th Armored Division has scorned a nickname.

Let the other outfits give themselves tricky, blood-curdling, or humorous nicknames, but not the 4th Armored. All the way down the line, from the big brass to the buck private, the men feel that "4th Armored" is sufficient.

Nevertheless, the 4th Armored Division does have a nickname. It was thrust on the Division by outsiders who fought along with it in France, Germany and Czechoslovakia. It is known as the "Breakthrough" Division. It hammered and slammed at Nazi defenses from the time of the Normandy invasion until the collapse of the Wehrmacht, and it never failed to break through.

There is one name that will always be associated with the 4th Armored.

Bastogne!

The 101st Airborne Division had been surrounded at Bastogne by the Nazis' last great counteroffensive. The acting commander of the 101st had thrilled the Allied world by his reply of "Nuts!" to the German demand to surrender or be destroyed. The desperate troops of the Airborne outfit, subjected to a merciless pounding, had to have help. Someone had to break through the German ring of steel and men and effect their rescue.

166

Four medium tanks from the 4th Armored rolled up to a forest-lined roadway, all guns firing. The commander of the lead tank unbuttoned the turret and called to the worn soldiers in a ditch: "It's all right, boys—this is the 4th Armored."

"Hot damn, we're mighty glad to see you," the men of the Airborne division called from their positions. The contact with the heroic defenders of Bastogne was made by the 37th Tank Battalion and the 53d Armored Infantry Battalion.

After six months' training in England, the 4th Armored went into action in Normandy. It started breaking through from the day it landed. It played a key role in cutting off the Brittany peninsula, made a lightning sweep across France north of the Loire River, defended the Moselle bridgehead against crack panzer units, and made the first crossing of the Saare River.

The 4th Armored did not rest on its laurels after the brilliant rescue of the 101st at Bastogne. After Bastogne, the Division drove its way through the Eifel Mountains, secured the high ground over the Kyll River, and shelled and captured Bitburg. Then the "Breakthrough" outfit really shifted into high gear. In an all-out blitz it roared 65 miles in 48 hours, coming to a halt opposite Coblenz. Here the Division joined the Seventh Army and began a successful hunt for V-1 rocket launching sites.

Working with the Seventh Army, the 4th Armored crossed the Rhine near Worms and gave the territory in that vicinity a terrific pasting. It aided materially in the rapid advance of the Seventh Army by seizing intact a bridge across the Main River, and then drove on to Hanau, 10 miles east of Frankfurt-am-Main. Here the 4th Armored fought off numerous counterattacks by the heaviest German armor.

Six months after they had been in combat the men of the 4th Armored Division had received 1,959 decorations.

The 4th Armored moved so fast that it often stretched its supply lines to the breaking point. But it never slowed down. In one day it took 8,000 prisoners. At the close of the war the 4th Armored had joined the 90th Infantry Division and moved with it into Czechoslovakia.

5th Armored Division

THREE YEARS BEFORE IT PLUNGED into the battle for the liberation of Europe the 5th Armored Division officially adopted the nickname, "Victory" Division.

It was a wise choice, because when V-E Day came, the 5th Armored, after almost a year of bitter fighting, was the nearest American outfit to Berlin. It had fought its way from the beaches of Normandy, and the men and machines were ready for a crack at the capital of the Reich when the shattered German forces capitulated.

The Doughs of the 5th Armored will tell you that the month of fighting in the Hürtgen Forest and on the approaches to the Roer River was the most bitter they experienced. Held down by the terrain, weather and thousands of mines, the Tankers and Infantrymen fought a hacking, foot-by-foot battle. They lived in mud and rain and ice, and were constantly exposed to tremendous artillery concentrations. But this month of savage battle broke the German spirit. Never again did the Nazis fight with the ferocity they displayed at Hürtgen.

The "Victory" Division went into combat in August 1944. For the first time in the history of armored warfare a full armored division was to be sent driving through enemy territory in a spectacular 300-mile mission to disrupt and trap enemy forces. Fifteen days after the first 5th Armored tanks had rolled through the gap between Coutances and St.Lô, they had reached Argentan.

From here the 5th Armored turned east to cut off German units west of the Seine. Paris lay only 50 miles away, but the 5th swung north toward the junction of the Eure and Seine Rivers. In this natural pocket the Division trapped thousands of Nazis vainly attempting to cross the Seine and escape.

Paris liberated, the Victory Division started a fast drive to the Belgian border, 130 miles north. It cut through Compiègne Forest, crossed the Oise and Aisne Rivers, and then the Somme. A month later the Division was at Condé on the Belgian border.

New orders sent the outfit racing another 100 miles to the Meuse River. Speeding onward, the 5th Armored spearheaded the drive that liberated Luxembourg. On September 11, 1944, elements of the Victory Division crossed the Our River into Germany, and thus earned the distinction of being among the first Americans to fight on German soil.

In November the Victory Division, working with the 90th Infantry Division, crossed the Moselle River. Fighting hard in December during the "Bulge" period, the 5th Armored greeted 1945 by continuing to advance against the heaviest kind of opposition. At Coblenz, the 5th Armored smashed and then mopped up all enemy resistance.

By spring the 5th Armored Division had rolled to the Weser River, and in May, driving north of Brunswick, it reached the Elbe and crossed it. V-E Day found the Victory Division's sights set on Berlin.

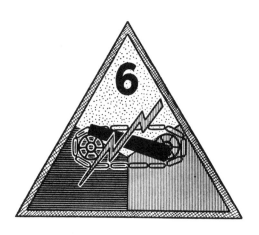

6th Armored Division

ARMORED DIVISIONS ARE SUPPOSED to be able to travel pretty fast, but few have eclipsed the speed records set in France in the summer of 1944 by the men of the 6th Armored, who called themselves the "Super 6th" and more than justified their claim to the name. Landing in Normandy on July 24, the 6th Armored put its tanks in high gear and headed for the coast of Brittany. In two weeks, the Division had pulled up at the outskirts of Brest, where its Combat Command A trapped 40,000 Germans and earned the nickname of the "Brassiere Boys." During its dash, the Super 6th averaged 25 miles a day, and in one 24-hour period covered 48 miles. It was that sort of fast traveling that prompted the division commander, Major General Robert W. Grow, to exclaim to one of his staff, "These maps are too small. Give me a map large enough so that I won't run off it today."

Leaving Brest to the Infantry, the Super 6th cruised on down to Lorient, and then turned east and rumbled through Orléans, Autun, Nancy, and Metz. Across France, at Dijon, it met up with the Seventh Army moving north from the Mediterranean, and pushed its way to the Saar River, within sight of Germany.

Then came the winter counteroffensive, and the 6th Armored was shifted to the south of the Ardennes, just north of Mersch,

Luxembourg, to relieve the 10th Armored. Five days later, it was in the thick of the action to the north of Bastogne. For 23 days, the Super 6th fought in the winter hell of the Bulge. Tank turrets froze, and tank doors wouldn't open. Rifle bolts got so stiff from the cold that they would operate only after being beaten with hand grenades. For five days, the Super 6th—now measuring distances in yards rather than miles—was pushed slowly back under the tremendous weight of the German assault. Then it held, and slowly the pendulum began to swing the other way, and the 6th Armored drove the enemy back.

The Germans threw everything they had at the Super 6th. Heavy artillery concentrations and barrages of rockets crashed incessantly, with tank and infantry forces charging behind them. Bombers blasted the 6th Armored from above. But the Division dug in, and by the time the enemy threat had been crushed, late in January, the Super 6th had pushed the Germans right across the Our River and back into their own country.

Then the American tankers began rolling again. Theirs wasn't all a war of machines, however. There was one sergeant, for instance—one among many like him—who, when his tanks were knocked out, seized a carbine, picked off 26 Jerries, and then, running out of ammunition, grabbed a submachine gun and shot three more. The men and machines of the 6th Armored added one more important page to their own military history when, on March 20, the Third and Seventh Armies were linked up by the junction of the 26th Infantry Division and the 6th Armored. By the time the Super 6th was through, it had convinced a lot of Nazis that maybe they weren't supermen after all.

7th Armored Division

ANYBODY WHO COULDN'T UNDERSTAND the need for gas rationing late in 1944 and 1945 might stop and reflect for a minute on the combat career of the 7th Armored Division. During nine months of action, from August to May, the "Lucky 7th"—just one of 15 armored divisions that saw action in the European Theater of Operations—used up 3,127,151 gallons of fuel, well over 10,000 gallons a day. And at that it ran out of gas.

It was at Verdun that the 7th Armored had to halt and wait for its fuel to catch up with it. Landing in Normandy on August 10, it set out in the direction of Chartres and, before it stopped, had covered 620 miles in its first 21 days in Europe, passing through Reims, Melun and Château-Thierry on the way.

The Lucky 7th really got around. It traveled nearly 2,000 miles, and served under four armies and eight corps. After being refueled at Verdun, it headed for Metz, and battered away at the outlying fortifications of that stronghold along with Doughboys of the 5th Infantry Division. Then the 7th Armored was transferred up to Holland, under the British Second Army.

On December 16, the 7th Armored Division was at St. Vith, when the Germans launched their counteroffensive in the Ardennes. For the next month, it fought furiously in the Battle of the Bulge, first losing ground and then grimly battling its way back into its former positions. After the Germans were thrown back, the Division got a brief rest, and then, late in March, came back to the front and broke out into Germany after crossing the Rhine at Remagen, where the 9th Armored had seized the bridge. Roaming unchecked in enemy territory, the Lucky 7th was ultimately assigned to reducing the Ruhr pocket. The Germans tried to make the job as uncomfortable as possible, even turning flak guns primarily used for antiaircraft against the advancing 7th Armored. But the Division was not fazed by this, and had the last say when, on April 16, it forced an entire panzer corps to surrender to it.

From the Ruhr, the 7th Armored journeyed north again, rejoining the British north of the Elbe and pointing its tanks toward the Baltic Sea. It had made a specialty of collecting German cities—Giessen, Hemer, Menden, Grevesmühlen and Dassow were among the ones it had taken—but now it began to specialize in collecting Germans. It began picking up so many prisoners that merely controlling the flow of its prisoner traffic became a problem, and at one time it had 51,000 in its camps. By the war's end, the 7th Armored Division's total bag of prisoners was computed at 113,042—not a bad return for the expenditure of fuel.

8th Armored Division

ONCE KNOWN AS THE "SHOW HORSE" DIVISION, the 8th Armored Division proved it was a work-horse outfit in the brief time it was in combat against the Nazi military machine.

It would have been in the fight against the Wehrmacht much sooner had it not been so valuable as a training division. Before it sailed for overseas on Election Day, 1944, the "Iron Snake," as it is now known, trained more than 50,000 officers and men, who were shipped abroad to fill gaps in eight other armored divisions.

When our tank forces took the severe mauling at Kasserine Pass, 4,000 trained replacements of the 8th Armored were shipped directly to Tunisia to help save the day, and launched the drive which pushed Rommel out of North Africa.

The 8th Armored reached France on January 4, 1945, and assembled in the Bacqueville area of upper Normandy. The German drive for Strasbourg brought a rush call for armor, and the division moved across France in the midst of a blizzard, skidding into Pont-à-Mousson three days and 350 miles later, only to find that the enemy thrust had been halted.

First taste of battle for the 8th Armored came in the Third Army's preliminary attack against the Moselle–Saar salient, Supporting the 94th Infantry Division, Combat Command A drove the crack 11th Panzer Division out of the fortress towns of Nennig, Berg and Sinz. The end of February found the 8th

174

Armored Division at Roermond, Holland, where it had been rushed secretly to relieve the British 7th Armored Division—part of the famed "Desert Rats" of Africa—and join the Ninth Army.

The Roer crossing was in progress, and Major General John M. Devine pushed the 8th Armored across to take Merbeck and Tetelrath. Combat Command B captured Lintfort and Rheinberg to clean up the west bank of the river, overcoming cross-fire from panzerfausts, mortars, burp guns, mines and antitank weapons. The men of the "Iron Snake," meeting opposition all the way, rolled through Ossenberg, Broth, Grunthal and Millingen, as the Germans fought to get all possible troops and equipment across the Rhine.

The Rhine crossing was made by the Division on March 27, all men and equipment crossing within 24 hours. The 8th Armored then took on the 116th Panzer Division in its drive toward Dorsten, keypoint of the northern flank of the then forming Ruhr River pocket. Plunging past Dorsten, the 8th Armored fought through Polsum, Kirchellen, Zweckel, Buer Massel and Kol Berlich, grinding down compressed German opposition.

Came a shift in Allied plans, and the 8th Armored drove toward Soest, taking Collinghausen, Nordert and Ebbinghausen. The Division fought on into Unna, near Dortmund, and then was pulled out of combat and sent rolling 100 miles to Wolfenbuttel. From there the 8th Armored moved farther south, and soon was massed around Blankenburg, at the foot of the Harz Mountains. Following heavy air and artillery attacks in the morning, the tank-infantry assault was made, and the city was captured before dark. This was the last major battle waged by the 8th Armored Division. After V-E Day, the division moved to Chotieschau, Czechoslovakia.

9th Armored Division

WITH THE POSSIBLE EXCEPTION of the titanic clash at El Alamein, no tank engagement in World War II will be longer remembered than the dashing armored coup which first put the American Army across the Rhine at Remagen bridge.

All Allied commanders—indeed, the world—applauded this bold action which was one of the major developments leading to the collapse of the German Army.

The 9th Armored accomplished this historic feat.

Striking with lightning speed, scorning all risks, the 9th Armored moved so swiftly that it had established a bridgehead before the Nazis could demolish the bridge or prepare defenses across the river.

Military authorities have estimated that the feat of the 9th Armored saved a minimum of 5,000 American dead and 10,000 wounded.

The 9th Armored, which was activated in 1942, was late in getting overseas. It crossed to England in August of 1944 and did not reach Normandy until a month later. But once on fighting soil it wasted no time. In six days after hitting France the 9th Armored was in Luxembourg near the German frontier.

Looked upon as a "Little Brother" by the bigger, older, and more experienced armored divisions such as the 1st, 2d and 3d Armored Divisions the 9th Armored proved it had what it takes when Rundstedt launched his mighty winter counteroffensive.

When the Nazis struck along the VIII Corps front the "Little Brother" 9th Armored, with no real combat experience, was the most powerful unit present to oppose the onslaught.

In its first real fight the Division's three combat commands were forced to fight on separate fronts. Command B made a six-day stand at St.Vith against superior strength. Command A fought ten days near Echternach, then, after an all night march without rest, launched its part in the operation that resulted in the breaking of the siege of Bastogne.

The third 9th combat command received a unit citation for its contribution to the epic of Bastogne. It stood up against the German juggernaut and delayed it for 36 hours, thus giving the 101st Airborne time to dig in for the defense of the city.

Proved in battle now, the 9th Armored was sent into the offensive between the Roer and Rhine Rivers. It couldn't be stopped. In seven smashing, driving days it rolled from river to river.

And then it electrified the world by its action at Remagen bridge.

After its crossing of the Rhine the 9th Armored raced to Limburg, brooking no opposition, and there released thousands of Allied prisoners of war.

Then the 9th turned east, serving as the spearhead of the First Army's thrust toward the Russian lines. In full cry now, the Division, no longer a "Little Brother," encircled Leipzig, paving the way for the fall of that key city.

The 9th Armored's final assignment was in the Sudetenland.

The 9th Armored Division was a little late getting into action, but once turned loose it never put on the brakes. It was in high all the time.

10th Armored Division

NOVEMBER 1, 1944, IS A MEMORABLE DAY for the "Tigers" of the 10th Armored Division. On that day the outfit began five busy months of combat during which it bagged 30,000 prisoners and took 450 cities and towns.

The Tiger Division didn't begin its overseas service until the war on the Western Front had been under way for three months, but the 10th got into action in time to establish its claim to three big "firsts":

First Third Army division to enter Germany.

First Third Army division to capture a major German city—Trier.

First Third Army division to stop the Germans at Bastogne during the Ardennes breakthrough.

It was Combat Command B of the Tigers that held out at Bastogne, side by side with the 101st Airborne, while Germans attacking from all sides tried to crush the American forces waiting for relief to come through from the outside.

The Tigers first growled in anger in the Metz–Nancy area, and subsequently fought at the Siegfried and Maginot Lines, in France, Belgium, Luxembourg, and Germany. During 12 crowded days that ended with the seizure of Trier, the 10th Armored cleared a good deal of the Saar–Moselle triangle, earning special praise from General Patton, crossed the Saar, captured Saarburg, took a total of 65 towns, and rounded up 10,000 prisoners, including 4,500 at Trier alone.

Toward the end of the war in Europe, the Tigers were shifted to the Seventh Army and lashed deep into southern Germany. They captured Neustadt, helped the 63d Division take the famous city of Heidelberg, and at Uffing, in Bavaria, made an unexpected catch of 300 Germans, including a handful of colonels in civilian clothes, who were hiding in the town despite posted signs saying that it was a neutral zone.

On V-E Day the Tigers were in the western part of the supposedly impregnable Southern Redoubt, where the Germans had boasted they would make a last, unbeatable stand. But the Tigers were no longer surprised by German plans gone awry. They remembered their capture of Neuschwanstein Castle, for instance, collection point for millions of dollars' worth of artistic loot the Nazis had stripped from all over Europe. At the castle, the 10th Armored came across a letter of directions from Hermann Goering, art-collector extraordinary, in which he advised his subordinates that he would use the whole Luftwaffe, if necessary, to transport captured treasures to Germany. No wonder the German Air Force didn't seem to know what it was doing.

The Tigers settled down for guard duty at Garmisch-Partenkirchen, scene of the 1932 winter Olympics.

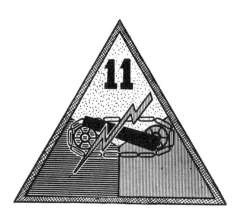

11th Armored Division

IT IS GENERALLY CONCEDED that thunderbolts travel pretty fast, but nobody ever suspected that a whole armored division of "Thunderbolts" could strike as quickly as the 11th Armored Division did in the winter of 1944-45.

The Thunderbolt Division (it shares the nickname with the 83d Infantry Division) was crossing the English Channel in mid-December, when Rundstedt launched his counteroffensive. The Allies were in desperate need of all the reinforcements they could get, and a brand-new armored division could mean a lot.

The 11th Armored hit the beaches of Normandy one morning and instantly set off on a forced march, skidding into Neufchâteau, Belgium, at midnight of the same night.

The next day—just 24 hours after hitting European soil for the first time—the Thunderbolts roared into action. They had a very definite mission: to get astride the vital Neufchâteau–Bastogne highway and prevent the Germans from gaining control of it. The 11th Armored jumped off in an attack, and the Germans had to revise any supply plans they had involving that critical highway.

Rarely in military history had an armored division gone into action so quickly from so far behind the lines.

Once started, the Thunderbolts kept on rumbling toward the heart of Europe. In January, they continued to fight in Belgium, and the next month, with the 6th Armored, they took Trois

Vierges and Goedange. They spearheaded the Allied drive across the Kyll River, fought through northern Luxembourg, and drove on to the Rhine, over-running Kirschweiler, Dochweiler and Winnweiler.

Swerving to the south, the Thunderbolts earned themselves new honors by becoming the first American unit to enter Austria. On their way, they paused long enough, west of Kaiserslautern, to help capture two German armies—the First and Seventh. In March, the Thunderbolts crossed the Rhine, drove toward Nürnberg, and sent two columns racing into Bavaria and finally joining up at Cham, 28 miles northeast of Regensburg and 1,200 feet high in the Alps. They captured Linz, on the Danube, and on V-E Day, were assembled at Früdenthal.

A few weeks later, while on occupation duty near Oberdonau, the Thunderbolts started reckoning up their combat achievements. In only a few months of action, they discovered, the 11th Armored had taken a total of 76,229 prisoners—an average of 600 a day and twice as many as were taken by the entire American Army during the last war.

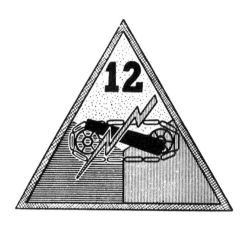

12th Armored Division

SOMEONE MUST HAVE TIED A CAN to the tails of the "Hellcats" of the 12th Armored Division when they rolled into Bavaria to tangle with crack troops and armor of the Nazi Army. For 37 days the men and machines of this slugging outfit lashed at the Wehrmacht without let-up, and at the finish had compiled an astounding combat record.

In this drive the Hellcats knocked most of Bavaria off the German-held map, conquering 22,000 square miles. They liberated 8,413 Allied prisoners of war (mostly Americans), and freed 20,000 slave laborers. But they captured prisoners even faster than they released them. When the 12th Armored had completed its drive through Bavaria, 63,000 Germans were enclosed in its barbed-wire stockades.

The outfit first hit combat in December 1944, near the Maginot Line in France. It helped in the closing of the Colmar pocket, and then swung north to the Siegfried Line. In hard fighting, it spearheaded the Third Army's drive for the encirclement of the Germans in the Saar, and then went back to the Seventh Army for the push across the Rhine.

Probably the Hellcats' biggest achievement—and it ranks with the top feats of the war—was the capture intact of a bridge across the Danube at Dillingen. This job was of tremendous help to the advance of the Seventh Army into Austria, allowing the Americans to pour men and supplies across the Danube in a ceaseless flow. Because of a garbled radio message to headquarters, this vital bridge came close to not being used. An officer radioed, "Have bridge of Danube, and it's blue." Somehow, the "blue" was changed to "blown" and headquarters was searching for another bridge when the correction came through.

A poll conducted by the *Hellcat News* revealed that the Doughs of the 12th Armored considered the capture of the Alsatian town of Herlisheim their toughest job.

It was in defense of this small village, situated on what 12th Armored Doughs and Tankers call "Purple Heart Plain" that the Division wrote the bloodiest chapter in its history. For 12 days the Hellcats fought two crack divisions, the 10th SS Panzer and the 553d Volksgrenadier. Wave after wave of German infantry and tank combinations smashed at the Hellcat front. The 12th Armored, barely a month in combat, repulsed them all.

For its part in sealing off the Colmar pocket, the 12th Armored was authorized by the French to wear the Colmar coat of arms, and many individual awards were made by the French to members of the division.

On March 17, the Hellcats jumped off near Trier to spearhead the Third Army's assault on the Rhineland. The Germans threw everything they could muster in defense, but the Hellcats reached the Rhine in three days, and in three more they occupied Ludwigshafen, Speyer and Germersheim.

Eight days later the 70th found itself as the point unit in the Seventh Army's drive across southern Germany. It was in this lightning strike that the Dillingen bridge was captured, providing an artery through which Allied troops flooded into southern Germany for the climactic campaign of the European war. The enemy tried everything to knock out the precious span, but the 12th Armored held it against aircraft and artillery attack until troops of the 3d Infantry Division arrived to take over the job.

The Hellcats then took to the trail, once again as the tip of the Seventh Army's flying wedge. With the Germans on the run, the 12th Armored captured airfields, planes, war factories, and thousands of prisoners. It liberated 2,800 prisoners from Landsberg Prison, where Hitler wrote *Mein Kampf*.

It took the 12th Armored but 37 days to clear a path from the Rhine to Austria.

13th Armored Division

THE 13TH ARMORED ("BLACK CAT") DIVISION was one of the last outfits to clear this country for overseas combat, but in the little time the Black Cats were in action they clawed and scratched and bedevilled the Nazis just as efficiently as any of the older and more experienced outfits.

The Black Cats didn't leave this country for the European Theater until late January 1945, and did not get into action against the Panzers until the closing stages of the Allied drive in southern Germany. Working with General Patton's Third Army, the Black Cats were part of the relentless surge that by-passed Berchtesgaden in the race to link up with the Russians. In this drive the men of the 13th Armored were never stopped, and fought with the skill and coolness of hardened veterans.

Late in April 1945, the 13th Armored was at Alterhofen, and shortly afterward the division was across the Danube River, east of Regensburg at a point two miles southeast of Straubing.

On May 2—less than a week before the Nazi capitulation— the 13th Armored Division had hammered its way to Adolf Hitler's birthplace, Braunau, five miles from the Inn River.

It was in this closing action that a platoon of Black Cats captured a German major who was so anxious to put himself in good light with the Yanks that he gave away the location of a Nazi general's headquarters. The Yanks rolled up to the place to investigate and made quite a profitable haul—two generals with their staffs.

The experience of Lieutenant Colonel Dale E. Means of Valier, Pennsylvania, an assistant chief of staff of the Black Cat Division, illustrates the coolness of the Cats in combat. Lieutenant Colonel Means was captured during the clearing out of Straubing, and held prisoner for four hours. He attempted to talk his captors into surrender. They refused. He then told them that his tanks and artillery would blow the town to bits. The Nazis again refused. Finally, the American said, "Let's see the mayor." The Nazis agreed, and the Colonel was OK, because he knew the office of the town's No. 1 man was already in Yank hands.

14th Armored Division

THE 14TH ARMORED IS NOT KNOWN AS THE "Liberator" Division for nothing.

It has earned that name.

In its more than 500 miles of ranging over Germany and Nazi-held territory the men and machines of the 14th Armored freed more than 20,000 Allied prisoners of war.

And it was poison to the German war machine.

The 14th Armored took upward of 50,000 German prisoners. It captured or destroyed 500 or more German tanks. It captured 100 self-propelled guns. It put 500 Nazi artillery pieces out of action. It overran and crushed 400 ack-ack guns. It captured or destroyed more than 1,000,000 small arms. More than 400 aircraft bearing the swastika fell to its antiaircraft guns, and it destroyed 50,000 tons of enemy munitions.

Nothing German was safe from the hurtling 14th. It captured 2,000 railroad cars and took intact 100 locomotives. It seized 200 factories and before the Nazi collapse it had liberated or captured 1,000 cities, towns and villages.

Activated at Camp Chaffee, Arkansas, in 1942, the 14th Armored Division was destined to fight with two armies in the liberation of Europe—the Seventh and Third.

The 14th Armored saw its first combat in the Vosges Mountains. Here it breached the Nazi defenses and poured out into the broad Alsatian plain, where it launched a drive from

Hagenau that culminated in the capture of Wissembourg and the crossing of the German frontier.

No armored division played a bigger part in thwarting Rundstedt's counteroffensive than did the 14th. It was largely due to the 14th's do-or-die stand that the Nazis' hope for overrunning Alsace and recapturing Strasbourg was foiled. For days the 14th Armored fought a terrific defensive battle against vastly superior strength.

At Hatten and Rittershofen the Germans threw three divisions—two panzer and one panzergrenadier—at the 14th Armored. The Division came out mauled and bloody, but Strasbourg, which hung in the balance during the melee, was not recaptured by the Nazis.

The 14th Armored again went on the offensive when it cracked the Siegfried Line at two places and drove to the Rhine at Germersheim. It rolled across the Rhine at Worms and captured Lohr, Bad Bruckenau, Neustadt and other towns. Then it swung south and liberated 5,000 prisoners at Hammelburg, and outflanked Bayreuth and Nürnberg. The 14th Armored then was transferred to Patton's Third Army. Teamed with the 86th Infantry Division, the 14th took Augsburg and drove to the infamous prison camp at Moosburg where 110,000 Allied prisoners were held.

The Americans gave the German garrison five hours in which to make an unconditional surrender. SS troops opened fire on the Yanks. Ninety minutes later the tanks of the 14th Armored were rolling through the prison camp.

In its last long dash the Liberators crossed the Danube and pushed to the Isar River. They were still rolling, still flattening the Nazis when the war ended.

16th Armored Division

THE 16TH ARMORED DIVISION averaged 8,000 prisoners per day while it was in combat.

But it was only in combat one day.

That will always be a memorable day for the men of the 16th. Swarming into Pilsen, Czechoslovakia, after long moves across the continent of Europe, the 16th Armored decisively captured the city famed both for its beer and as the seat of the Skoda munitions works.

There was only one jarring note to the last-minute triumph. Allied bombers, seeking out the Skoda plants, had inadvertently hit the beer factories as well.

The 16th Armored arrived in France on February 5, 1945, and was subsequently assigned to the Third Army. Traveling to Nürnberg, the division got there on April 28 for final precombat training. On May 4 it leaped to Waidhaus, 80 miles away, and two days later launched its attack on the beer city, at the far end of the American line of penetration into Czechoslovakia.

After its brief flurry of combat, the 16th Armored had the trying job of herding together German soldiers and civilians attempting to flee from the Russian forces in Prague.

One well remembered tank of the 16th Armored never did fight at all. Separated from the division in France when the railroad car on which it was lashed had to be side-tracked, the tank and the crew set out determinedly to rejoin their outfit. The tank men raced from France to Belgium, into Luxembourg and Germany, and on into Czechoslovakia. Finally they rumbled into Pilsen.

But by the time they got there the war had ended.

20th Armored Division

MAJOR GENERAL ORLANDO WARD was in action during only a few months of the European War, but he saw its beginning and its end. Arriving in North Africa in November 1942, with the 1st Armored Division, he was wounded in Tunisia the following April, and returned to the United States. Just two years later, he came back to action as commanding general of the 20th Armored, one of the last American divisions to be committed to battle in the European Theater of Operations.

The 20th Armored had made itself felt long before it went overseas. Thousands of men trained in its ranks had been shipped to Europe and assigned to other fighting units as armored replacements.

But not until April 1945, did the Division get a chance to do some fighting under its own colors. Then it turned up on the Seventh Army front in southern Germany, as part of the force advancing on Munich. On its way, smashing into Salzburg just behind spearheading elements of the 3d Infantry Division, the 20th Armored bagged a banner crop of high-ranking Nazis, including three lieutenant generals, a major general, and Dr. Paul Schmidt, chief of the Press Department of the German Foreign Office.

Herr Dr. Schmidt was an especially rich find. When he was nabbed, he had with him a brief case containing 85,000 German marks and 1,000 kroner.

After swinging south of Munich to cut off German escape routes from the falling city, the 20th Armored Division moved into an area north of Lake Chiem and, in June, was stationed at Traunstein, Germany.

When the 20th's commander left the front, in 1943, the vaunted Afrika Korps was still very much in action, and the Allies were still wincing from the blows they had taken in such battles as Kasserine Pass. When he got back, there was no Afrika Korps, and there were very few corps of any kind doing anything but moving backward fast, or surrendering. It was a contrast any American would have enjoyed.

APPENDIX I

ORDER OF BATTLE OF U.S. FORCES

(The order of battle of our Allies is not shown below army level, except to show
U.S. divisions under their operational control)

European Theater of Operations

(As of May 7, 1945)

Unit	Commander
SUPREME HEADQUARTERS ALLIED EXPEDITIONARY FORCES	GENERAL OF THE ARMY D. D. EISENHOWER
Northern Group of Armies (21st Army Group)	F.M. Sir Bernard L. Montgomery
Canadian First Army	General H. D. G. Crerar
British Second Army	Lt.Gen. Sir Miles C. Dempsey
XVIII Corps (Airborne)	Maj.Gen. Matthew B. Ridgway
5 Armored Division	Maj.Gen. L. E. Oliver
7 Armored Division	Maj.Gen. R. W. Hasbrouck
82 Airborne Division	Maj.Gen. James M. Gavin
8 Infantry Division	Maj.Gen. Bryant E. Moore
Central Group of Armies (12th Army Group)	General Omar N. Bradley
U.S. Ninth Army	Lt.Gen. William H. Simpson
XIII Corps	Maj.Gen. Alvan C. Gillem, Jr.
35 Infantry Division	Maj.Gen. Paul W. Baade
84 Infantry Division	Maj.Gen. A. R. Bolling
102 Infantry Division	Maj.Gen. Frank A. Keating

Unit	Commander
XVI Corps	Maj.Gen. John B. Anderson
29 Infantry Division	Maj.Gen. Charles H. Gerhardt
75 Infantry Division	Maj.Gen. Ray E. Porter
79 Infantry Division	Maj.Gen. Ira T. Wyche
95 Infantry Division	Maj.Gen. Harry L. Twaddle
XIX Corps	Maj.Gen. Raymond S. McLain
2 Armored Division	Maj.Gen. Isaac D. White
8 Armored Division	Maj.Gen. John M. Devine
30 Infantry Division	Maj.Gen. Leland S. Hobbs
83 Infantry Division	Maj.Gen. Robert C. Macon
U.S. First Army	Gen. Courtney H. Hodges
78 Infantry Division	Maj.Gen. Edward P. Parker, Jr.
VII Corps	Lt.Gen. J. Lawton Collins
3 Armored Division	Brig.Gen. Doyle O. Hickey
9 Infantry Division	Maj.Gen. Louis A. Craig
69 Infantry Division	Maj.Gen. Emil F. Reinhardt
104 Infantry Division	Maj.Gen. Terry M. Allen
VIII Corps	Maj.Gen. Troy H. Middleton
6 Armored Division	Brig.Gen. George W. Read, Jr.
76 Infantry Division	Maj.Gen. William R. Schmidt
87 Infantry Division	Maj.Gen. Frank L. Culin, Jr.
89 Infantry Division	Maj.Gen. Thomas D. Finley
U.S. Third Army	Gen. George S. Patton, Jr.
4 Infantry Division	Maj.Gen. Harold W. Blakeley
70 Infantry Division	Maj.Gen. Allison J. Barnett

Unit	Commander
III Corps	Maj.Gen. James A. Van Fleet
14 Armored Division	Maj.Gen. Albert C. Smith
99 Infantry Division	Maj.Gen. Walter E. Lauer
V Corps	Maj.Gen. Clarence R. Huebner
9 Armored Division	Maj.Gen. John W. Leonard
16 Armored Division	Brig.Gen. John L. Pierce
1 Infantry Division	Maj.Gen. Clift Andrus
2 Infantry Division	Maj. Gen. Walter M. Robertson
97 Infantry Division	Brig.Gen. Milton B. Halsey
XII Corps	Maj.Gen. S. LeRoy Irwin
4 Armored Division	Maj.Gen. William M. Hoge
11 Armored Division	Maj.Gen. Holmes E. Dager
5 Infantry Division	Maj.Gen. Albert E. Brown
26 Infantry Division	Maj.Gen. Willard S. Paul
90 Infantry Division	Maj.Gen. Herbert L. Earnest
XX Corps	Lt.Gen. Walton H. Walker
13 Armored Division	Maj.Gen. John Milliken
65 Infantry Division	Maj.Gen. Stanley E. Reinhart
71 Infantry Division	Maj.Gen. Willard G. Wyman
80 Infantry Division	Maj.Gen. Horace L. McBride
U.S. Fifteenth Army	Lt.Gen. Leonard T. Gerow
66 Infantry Division	Maj.Gen. Herman F. Kramer
106 Infantry Division	Maj.Gen. Donald A. Stroh
XXII Corps	Maj.Gen. Ernest N. Harmon
17 Airborne Division	Maj.Gen. William M. Miley
94 Infantry Division	Maj.Gen. Harry J. Malony

Unit	Commander
XXIII Corps	Maj.Gen. Hugh J. Gaffey
28 Infantry Division	Maj.Gen. Norman D. Cota
Southern Goup of Armies (6th Army Group)	Gen. Jacob L. Devers
U.S. Seventh Army	Lt.Gen. Alexander M. Patch
12 Armored Division	Maj.Gen. Roderick R. Allen
63 Infantry Division	Maj.Gen. Louis E. Hibbs
45 Infantry Division	Maj.Gen. Robert T. Frederick
100 Infantry Division	Maj.Gen. Withers A. Burress
XXI Corps	Maj.Gen. Frank W. Milburn
101 Airborne Division	Maj.Gen. Maxwell D. Taylor
36 Infantry Division	Maj.Gen. John E. Dahlquist
XV Corps	Lt.Gen. Wade H. Haislip
20 Armored Division	Maj.Gen. Orlando Ward
3 Infantry Division	Maj.Gen. John W. O'Daniel
42 Infantry Division	Maj.Gen. Harry J. Collins
86 Infantry Division	Maj.Gen. Harris M. Melasky
VI Corps	Maj.Gen. Edward H. Brooks
10 Armored Division	Maj.Gen. W. H. H. Morris, Jr.
44 Infantry Division	Maj.Gen. William F. Dean
103 Infantry Division	Maj.Gen. Anthony C. McAuliffe
SHAEF Reserve	
First Allied Airborne Army	Lt.Gen. Lewis H. Brereton
13 Airborne Division	Maj.Gen. Elbridge G. Chapman, Jr.

195

Mediterranean Theater of Operations

(As of May 2, 1945)

Unit	Commander
15th Army Group	Gen. Mark W. Clark
U.S. Fifth Army	Lt.Gen. Lucian K. Truscott
II Corps	Lt.Gen. Geoffrey Keyes
10 Mountain Division	Maj.Gen. George P. Hays
85 Infantry Division	Maj.Gen. John B. Coulter
88 Infantry Division	Maj.Gen. Paul W. Kendall
IV Corps	Maj.Gen. W. D. Crittenberger
1 Armored Division	Maj.Gen. Vernon E. Prichard
34 Infantry Division	Maj.Gen. Charles L. Bolté
92 Infantry Division	Maj.Gen. Edward M. Almond
British Eighth Army	Lt.Gen. Sir. R. L. McCreery
91 Infantry Division	Maj.Gen. William G. Livesay

Pacific Theater

(As of August 14, 1945)

GHQ. U.S. ARMY FORCES IN THE PACIFIC	GENERAL OF THE ARMY DOUGLAS MACARTHUR
U.S. Sixth Army	Gen. Walter Krueger
40 Infantry Division	Brig.Gen. Donald J. Myers
11 Airborne Division	Maj.Gen. Joseph M. Swing
I Corps	Maj.Gen. Innis P. Swift
25 Infantry Division	Maj.Gen. Charles L. Mullins
33 Infantry Division	Maj.Gen. Percy W. Clarkson
41 Infantry Division	Maj.Gen. Jens A. Doe

Unit		Commander
IX Corps	. . . .	Maj.Gen. Charles W. Ryder
77 Infantry Division	. . . .	Maj.Gen. Andrew D. Bruce
81 Infantry Division	. . . .	Maj.Gen. Paul J. Mueller
XI Corps	. . . .	Lt.Gen. Charles P. Hall
43 Infantry Division	. . . .	Maj.Gen. Leonard F. Wing
Americal Division	. . . .	Maj.Gen. William H. Arnold
1 Cavalry Division	. . . .	Maj.Gen. William C. Chase
U.S. Eighth Army	. . . .	Lt.Gen. R. L. Eichelberger
93 Infantry Division	. . . .	Maj.Gen. Harry H. Johnson
96 Infantry Division	. . . .	Maj.Gen. James L. Bradley
X Corps	. . . .	Maj.Gen. Franklin C. Sibert
24 Infantry Division	. . . .	Maj.Gen. Roscoe B. Woodruff
31 Infantry Division	. . . .	Maj.Gen. Clarence A. Martin
XIV Corps	. . . .	Lt.Gen. Oscar W. Griswold
6 Infantry Division	. . . .	Maj.Gen. Charles E. Hurdis
32 Infantry Division	. . . .	Maj.Gen. William H. Gill
37 Infantry Division	. . . .	Maj.Gen. Robert S. Beightler
38 Infantry Division	. . . .	Maj.Gen. Frederick A. Irving
U.S. Tenth Army	. . . .	Gen. Joseph W. Stilwell
XXIV Corps	. . . .	Lt.Gen. John R. Hodge
7 Infantry Division	. . . .	Maj.Gen. Archibald V. Arnold
27 Infantry Division	. . . .	Maj.Gen. George W. Griner
U.S. Army Forces, Middle Pacific	. . .	Lt.Gen. Robert C. Richardson, Jr.
98 Infantry Division	. . . .	Maj.Gen. Arthur M. Harper

197

APPENDIX II

CAMPAIGNS AND BATTLES, U.S. ARMY, 1941-45

Battle participation stars have been awarded for the following campaigns. Battle participation credit for the campaigns noted by asterisks may be awarded by the appropriate theater commander to units or individuals who actually engaged the enemy in the combat zone after the closing date.

European - African - Middle Eastern Theater

Egypt-Libya	June 11, 1942 to February 12, 1943
Air Offensive: Europe	July 4, 1942 to June 5, 1944
Algeria-French Morocco	November 8 to 11, 1942
Tunisia: Air	November 8, 1942 to May 13, 1943
Ground	November 17, 1942 to May 13, 1943
Sicily: Air	May 14 to August 17, 1943
Ground	July 9 to August 17, 1943
Naples-Foggia: Air	August 18, 1943 to January 21, 1944
Ground	September 9, 1943 to January 21, 1944
Rome-Arno	January 22 to September 9, 1944
Normandy	June 6 to July 24, 1944
Northern France	July 25 to September 14, 1944
Southern France	August 15 to September 14, 1944
North Apennines	September 10, 1944 to April 4, 1945
Rhineland	September 15, 1944 to March 21, 1945
Ardennes	December 16, 1944 to January 25, 1945
Central Europe	March 22 to May 11, 1945
Po Valley	April 5 to May 8, 1945

Asiatic - Pacific Theater

Central Pacific	December 7, 1941 to December 6, 1943
Burma	December 7, 1941 to May 26, 1942
Philippine Islands	December 7, 1941 to May 10, 1942
East Indies	January 1 to July 22, 1942
India-Burma	April 2, 1942 to January 28, 1945
Air Offensive: Japan	April 17, 1942 to September 2, 1945
Aleutian Islands	June 3, 1942 to August 24, 1943
China Defensive	July 4, 1942 to May 4, 1945
China Offensive	May 5, 1945 to September 2, 1945
Papua	July 23, 1942 to January 23, 1943
Guadalcanal	August 7, 1942 to February 21, 1943
New Guinea	January 24, 1943 to December 31, 1944°
Northern Solomons	February 22, 1943 to November 21, 1944°
Eastern Mandates: Air	December 7, 1943 to April 16, 1944°
Ground	January 31 to June 14, 1944°
Bismarck Archipelago	December 15, 1943 to November 27, 1944°
Western Pacific: Air	April 17, 1944 to September 2, 1945
Ground	June 15, 1944 to September 2, 1945
Southern Philippines	October 17, 1944 to July 4, 1945°
Luzon	January 9, 1945 to July 4, 1945°
Central Burma	January 29, 1945 to July 15, 1945
Ryukyus	March 26, 1945 to July 2, 1945

199

MAPS

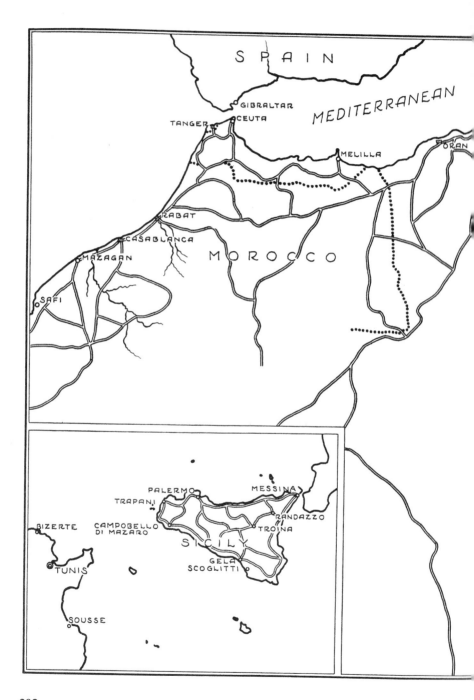

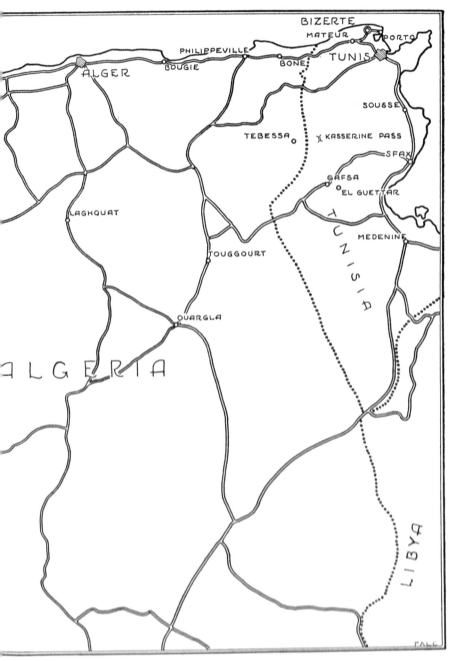

Map 1: North Africa and Sicily

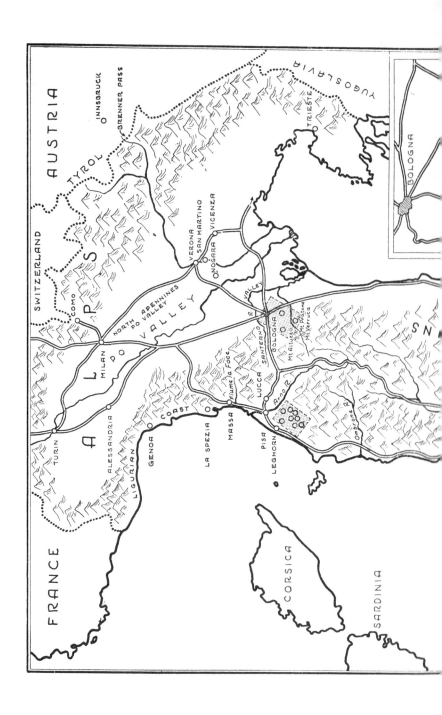

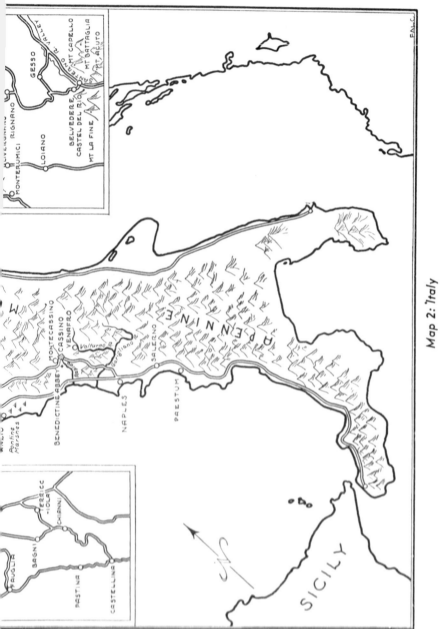

Map 2: Italy

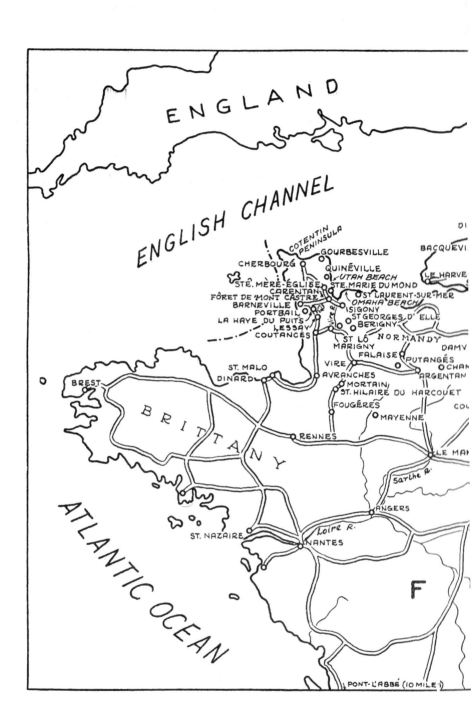

ENGLAND

ENGLISH CHANNEL

COTENTIN PENINSULA

DI

BACQUEVI

GOURBESVILLE

CHERBOURG

QUINÉVILLE

LE HARVE

UTAH BEACH

STE. MÈRE-ÉGLISE

STE. MARIE DU MOND

CARENTAN

FÔRET DE MONT CASTRE

ST LAURENT-SUR-MER

OMAHA BEACH

BARNEVILLE

ISIGONY

PORTBAIL

ST GEORGES D' ELLE

LA HAYE DU PUITS

BERIGNY

LESSAY

COUTANCES

ST LÔ

NORMANDY

MARIGNY

DAMV

FALAISE

PUTANGÉS

VIRE

CHAN

ST. MALO

AVRANCHES

ARGENTAN

DINARD

MORTAIN

ST. HILAIRE DU HARCOUET

BREST

FOUGÈRES

COU

MAYENNE

BRITTANY

RENNES

LE MAN

Sarthe R.

ANGERS

ATLANTIC OCEAN

ST. NAZAIRE

NANTES

Loire R.

F

PONT-L'ABBÉ (10 MILE)

206

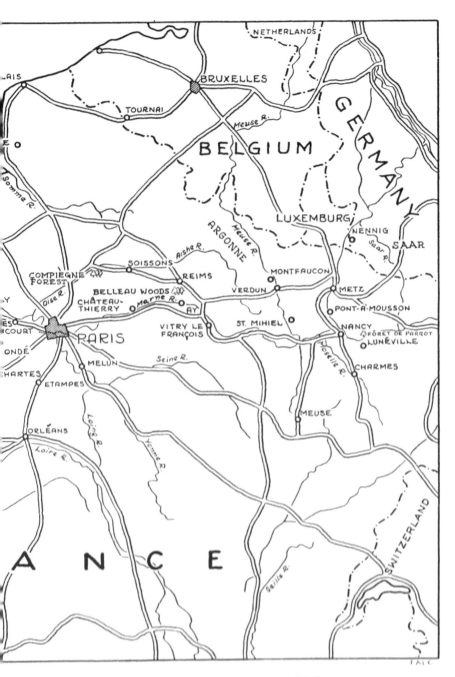

Map 3: Northern France and Belgium

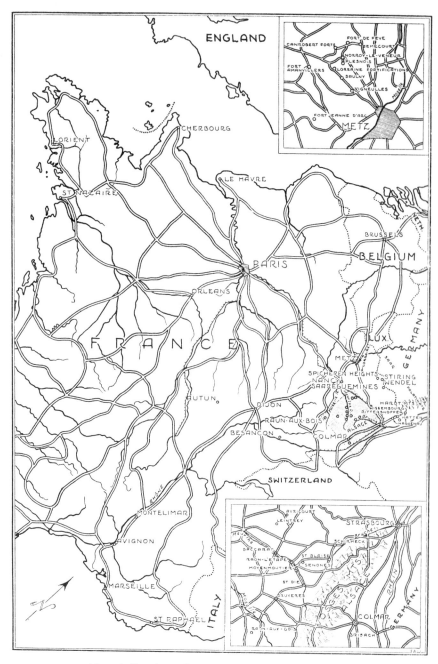

Map 4: Southern France and the Saar Palatinate

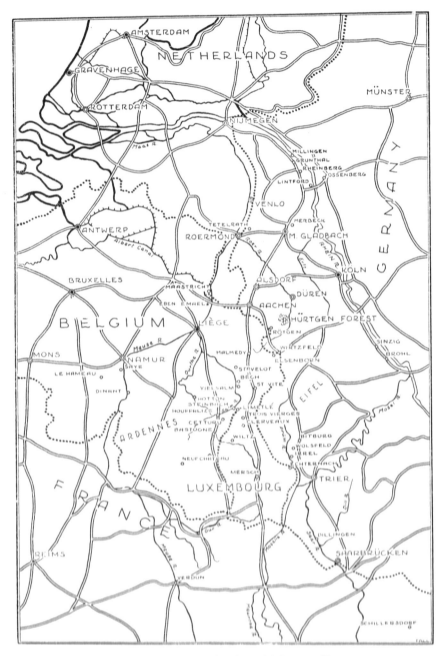

Map 5: Belgium, Netherlands and Western Germany

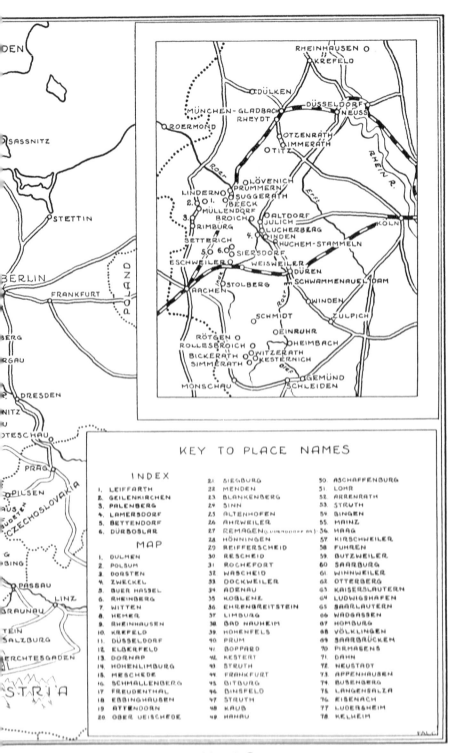

Map 6: Germany

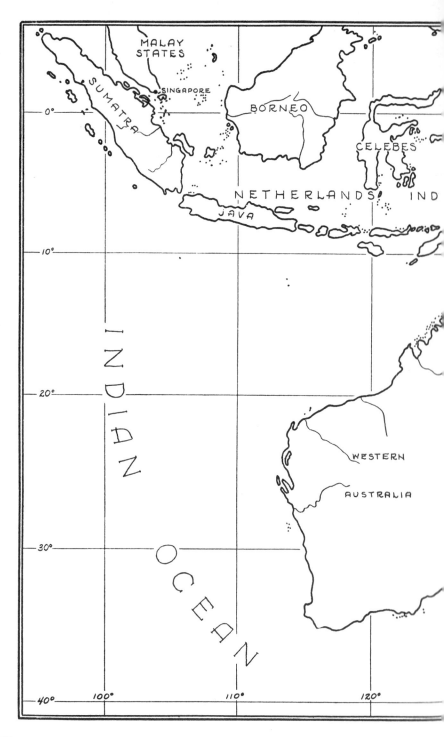

Map 7: Southwest Pacific

213

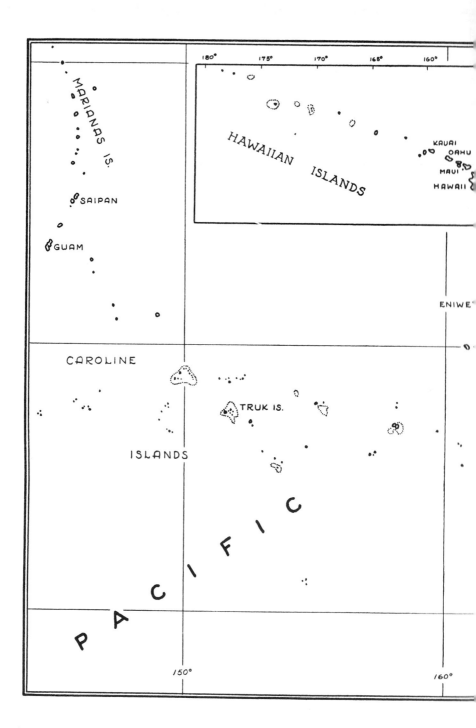

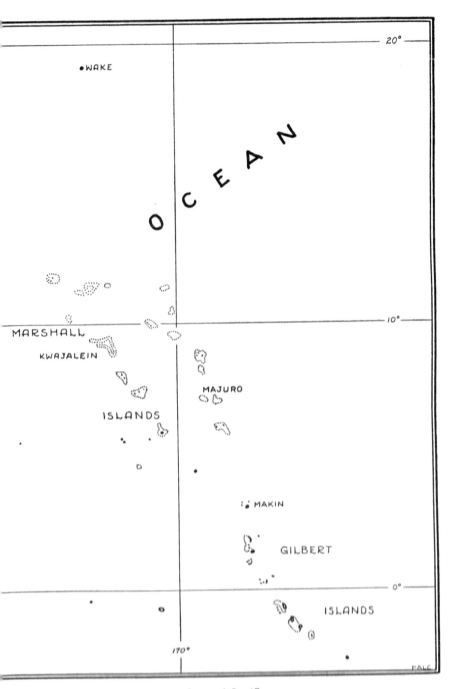

Map 8: Central Pacific

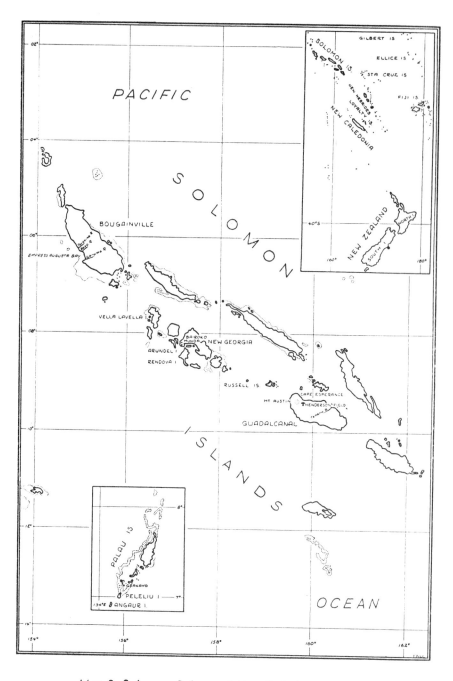

Map 9: Solomon, Palau and New Caledonia groups

216

PHILIPPINE
SEA

PHILIPPINES

LUZON

PORO
LINGAYEN GULF   GALIANO
ASINGAY DORSIN
 ROSARIO GAGUIO
CALASIAO
CALIMAY   BALETE PASS
LINGAYEN   BINALONAN
   HIGHWAY 8
ZAMBALES MTS   MUÑOZ
   TARLAC
   SAN MANUEL
CAMP O'DONNELL   BAMBAN DE
   FORT STOTSENBURG
   CLARK FIELD
OLONGAPO   ZIGZAG PASS
   BALANGA
   PILAR MARIVELES
SUBIC BAY   MANILA
BAGAC   FT MCKINLEY
BATAAN PEN   NICHOLS FIELD
MARIVELES   TAGAYTAY RIDGE
CORREGIDOR   IMUS
CABCABEN   ROSARIO
FT DRUM   LOS BAÑOS
HIGHWAY 17   SAN PABLO

LUBANG   PARAÑON
   VERDE
   MARINDUQUE

MINDORO   SIMARA   BURIAS
   ROMBLON   TICAO
   SAMAR
   CARABAO
   MASBATE

PANAY
   BIAS PASS
   ORMOC   TACLOBAN
ILOILO   CAMOTES IS   PALOMPON
   BACOLOD   BURAUEN
GUIMARAS   CEBU   DULAG
   ABUYOG
   LEYTE
PALAWAN   BOHOL
NEGROS

SULU SEA   MINDANAO
   MARAMAG

NORTH
BORNEO   BASILAN

TAWITAWI
   SULU ARCHIPELAGO

Map 10: The Philippines

217

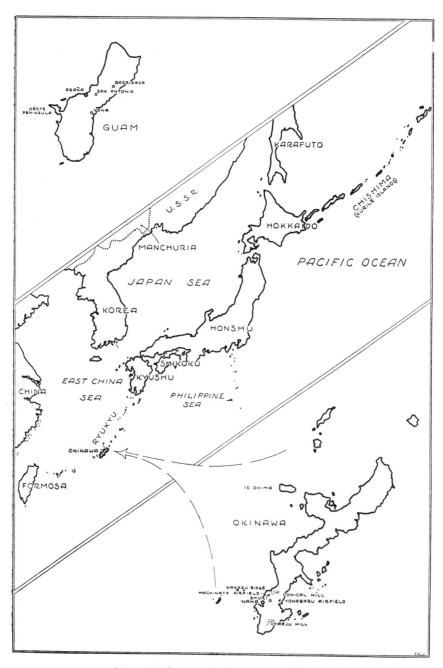

Map 11: Guam, the Ryukyus and Japan